I.W. THOMPSON .

DUTCH INLAND SAILING PILOT

*Other cruising guides and pilots
published by Stanford Maritime*

Baltic Southwest Pilot
by Mark Brackenbury

Brittany and Channel Islands
Cruising Guide
by David Jefferson

Cruising French Waterways
by Hugh McKnight

Frisian Pilot: Den Helder to
the Kiel Canal
by Mark Brackenbury

Norwegian Cruising Guide
by Mark Brackenbury

Scottish West Coast Pilot:
Troon to Ullapool, and the
Inner Hebrides
by Mark Brackenbury

Bristol Channel and Severn Pilot
by Peter Cumberlidge

Stanford's River Thames
A Companion and Boating Guide
by Graham Hayward

DUTCH INLAND SAILING PILOT

Henry Levison

STANFORD MARITIME LIMITED · LONDON

Stanford Maritime Limited
59 Grosvenor Street London W1X9DA

British Library Cataloguing in Publication Data

Levison, Henry
    Dutch inland sailing pilot.
    1. Netherlands. Inland waterways. Pilot's guides
    I. Title
    623.89′229492

    ISBN 0-540-07432-2

Typeset by Tameside Filmsetting Limited,
Ashton-under-Lyne, Lancashire
Printed in Great Britain by BAS Printers Limited,
Over Wallop, Hampshire

Contents

Acknowledgements

I wish to thank my wife, and all who have crewed with us on our Netherlands holidays, for their help and encouragement which led to the preparation of this book. For the photographs which illustrate the cruising grounds, I am indebted to Keith Fenton, Bryan Herve, Ken Herve, Alan Holland, Dr Gil Rattner and Harry Stapleton. I also wish to thank: Anne Chandler MA for her help with geographical material; Mark Brackenbury for his most constructive and helpful criticism of the manuscript; Phoebe Mason and Adrian Morgan at Stanford Maritime for their advice and co-operation throughout the production stages.

By the same author: Astro-Navigation by Calculator (David & Charles)

Introduction

This book has been written to fill a gap in the range of sailing guides. Whereas other books cover the coast and ports of entry to the Netherlands, little has been published in English on where to go after arrival. The aim of this book is to fill this gap, and describe the inland sailing areas open to fixed-mast yachts in our nearest and best expanse of sheltered waters. The Frisian Islands and sea passages to the coast are not included as they are well covered in the books listed in Chapter 1.

The cruising grounds are grouped and described in sections corresponding to Dutch charts, thus allowing readers to refer directly from book to appropriate chart and vice versa. The maps here are not to be used for navigation: their purpose is solely orientation and to illustrate the text. This guide is not meant to be a substitute for charts; its purpose is to provide practical information about the inland routes and places passed, together with some historical background. It is essential to possess the appropriate Dutch charts for cruising the Netherlands; for this reason no attempt has been made to illustrate channels or harbours as they are all shown there in perfect detail, and no yachtsman should attempt a passage without them.

Opening times of bridges and locks for the summer months are given throughout in Dutch local time, and were correct at the time of writing. However, they are subject to alteration from year to year and should only be used as a guide. A current issue of the Almanak mentioned in Chapter 1 should be used to check these times. Some useful Dutch words are given in the text and summarised in the Glossary at the end of the book.

Fig. 1   Cruising grounds

CHAPTER 1

Cruising in the Netherlands

For safe and enjoyable family cruising with a fixed-mast yacht, the Netherlands are probably unique in their richness of variety, charm, interest, facilities and friendliness. Language is rarely a barrier as most people speak very good English. In fact, it is the author's experience that many Dutch yachtsmen speak better English than their visitors. Before proceeding any further, readers are reminded that the Netherlands is the correct name of the country popularly known as 'Holland'. Although the Dutch are very tolerant of their visitors, all foreigners are urged to refer to the country as the Netherlands and not Holland: the latter comprises the provinces of North and South Holland, which form only part of the kingdom of the Netherlands.

The Netherlands provide no escape from a British summer. Weather patterns are similar in both countries and may be summarised as changeable: usually from bad to worse. However, this is compensated for by the vast inland areas of sheltered water. They permit safe, dry sailing in wind conditions which would confine family cruisers to their moorings in British waters. However, even sheltered waters can become quite choppy in severe conditions, and newcomers to the Netherlands should not expect a smooth passage all the time. Weather forecasts (weerberichten) in English are broadcast from Scheveningen. Times and frequencies are given in Dutch chart books and the British and Dutch almanacs; they are also obtainable from VHF port radio stations.

All foreign vessels entering Dutch waters are obliged to report their arrival to the nearest Customs office, and not wait for the officers to contact them. A fine of 250 guilders (about £75) can be imposed for failing to report your arrival. There are Customs posts at Breskens, Flushing, Roompot lock, Hook of Holland, Scheveningen, IJmuiden, Den Helder, Harlingen, Vlieland, Terschelling, Lauwersoog and Delfzijl. If duty-free supplies are obtained en route to the Netherlands, ensure that you do not have more than the EEC allowance or you will have to pay duty on the excess. You must be able to produce a VHF radio operator's licence if the yacht is so equipped. The Dutch word for customs is *Douane*.

Cruising Grounds

All the inland waterways of the Netherlands are used by commercial craft; and where these can go, yachts may go too. But remember that commercial craft have priority over pleasure craft. Always give way to them. In the busiest waterways yachts must keep to the starboard side and should have their engines ready for immediate use, as tacking, or too slow a speed, may impede the safe passage of commercial craft. Depths in the waterways, harbours and marinas are generally sufficient for yachts with a draught of 2 m, but special mention is given of places where depths are less than 2 m.

An inland passage between France and the Baltic is possible via the French, Belgian, Dutch and German canals, but only in the Netherlands is it possible to traverse the whole country with a fixed mast. Routes to Belgium and France are covered in Chapter 3, and to Germany in Chapter 12.

The cruising areas *(fig. 1)* comprise Zeeland, South Holland, North Holland, the IJsselmeer and Friesland. Any one of them can be visited in a fortnight's holiday from the English east or south coast sailing centres, but several such fortnights are necessary to explore one thoroughly.

Zeeland is the nearest province for most British and Belgian yachts and is conveniently entered at Flushing. It contains many of the best places to visit: Middelburg, Veere, Veerse Meer, Zierikzee and Goes.

South Holland extends from the Haringvliet through Dordrecht, Rotterdam, Gouda and Leiden to the bulbfields. The canal routes from Zeeland to Amsterdam pass through this province.

The province of North Holland covers Haarlem, Amsterdam, Alkmaar, Den Helder and the whole of the western shore of the IJsselmeer. The north-eastern shore is part of Friesland, the district of lakes and a chain of offshore islands that continues east into German waters.

Books

North Sea Passage Pilot by Brian Navin. A detailed account of routes from the English coast (Dover to Cromer) across the traffic lanes to the Continent between Calais and Den Helder. Covers all the Channel and North Sea passages to the Dutch coast.

North Sea Harbours and Pilotage by Jack Coote. Covering the French, Belgian and Dutch coasts from Calais to Den Helder, it will suffice for entry to all the sailing grounds described in this book.

Frisian Pilot by Mark Brackenbury. Gives a comprehensive coverage of the Dutch and German Frisian Islands and the adjacent coasts from Den Helder to the Kiel Canal.

Almanak Voor Watertoerisme, deel 2. This annual Dutch publication covers in minute detail every place in the Netherlands accessible to boats. It is a treasure of invaluable information which cannot be matched by any other book. Unfortunately there is no English version, but the most important information such as opening times of bridges and locks, bridge clearances, VHF channels, fuel and water supplies can be understood without any knowledge of Dutch. It includes tide tables and differences based on Flushing, Hook of Holland and Harlingen. Furthermore, it also covers Belgium, providing similar information for Nieuwpoort, Ostend, Blankenberge, Zeebrugge, Antwerp, Bruges and Ghent, and many others beyond the scope of this book. The Almanak can be purchased from chart agents in Britain but is obtainable more cheaply and easily from any bookshop or chandlery at the first port of call in the Netherlands.

It is not possible to use the Almanak to best advantage without some knowledge of Dutch, but certain headings recur throughout and if their meanings are known it is usually possible to derive the required information. Some of the most useful words are:

Aanlegplaatsen	temporary berthing places
Ligplaatsen	overnight berths
Jachthaven	yacht harbour, marina
Havenmeester	harbourmaster
Bediening	opening times of bridges and locks
ma. t/m zat	Monday through Saturday
zo. en fd.	Sundays and public holidays
di, wo, do, vr	Tuesday, Wednesday, Thursday, Friday
gesloten	closed
Bruggen	bridges (singular: *brug*)
hoog	vertical clearance
spoorbrug	railway bridge
verkeersbrug	road bridge
vaste brug	fixed bridge
beweegbare brug, ophaalbrug, hefbrug, basculebrug, draaibrug, pontonbrug, vlotbrug	opening bridges, of different types (as described on page 14/15)
Gat	channel
Sluis	lock (plural: *sluizen*)
Kanaal	canal
Motorbrandstof	fuel
die.	diesel
be.	petrol (*benzine*)
Bootmotorherstellers	engine repairs
Werven	boat yards
Hefkraan	crane
Zeilmaker	sailmaker
Marifoon	VHF radiotelephone
kanaal	radio channel
Wassalon	launderette
Wasgelegenheid	washing facilities
Douches	showers

A glossary of useful Dutch words is at the end of this book.

Charts

There is no need to use any British charts once the Continental coast has been reached. The excellent Dutch Hydrographic Service yacht charts *(Hydrografische Kaarten voor Kust- en Binnenwateren)* cover most of the sailing grounds in this book. They are bilingual productions with all explanations of chart symbols, abbreviations, harbour facilities, etc in Dutch and English. Bound as flexible books, their size is convenient for use in the cockpit, and clear waterproof covers are sold with them to protect against wear and tear.

The books contain a useful summary of facilities at every harbour: each page is a large-scale metric chart which includes inset plans of harbours, marinas and other mooring places; VHF channels for locks, bridges and port authorities; and the callsigns and frequencies of radio beacons.

This guide has been arranged in sections corresponding with the areas covered by the Dutch chart books and, where possible, in the order of the charts comprising each book. Like the Almanak already mentioned, they are best obtained on arrival in the Netherlands but can be purchased from chart agents in Britain. New editions are published annually. Those covered in this book are:

1801 Noordzeekust, Oostende tot Den Helder   Covers the coast from Ostend to Den Helder and will suffice for a coastal passage from Belgium into every possible place of entry to the Netherlands south of Den Helder.

1803 Westerschelde, Vlissingen tot Antwerpen en Kanaal van Terneuzen naar Gent   The West Schelde from Flushing to Antwerp; the commonest area for beginning a Netherlands cruise.

1805 Oosterschelde, Veerse Meer en Grevelingenmeer   The Veerse Meer and East Schelde form the nearest and most popular Dutch cruising ground for most British yachtsmen.

1807 Zoommeer, Volkerak en Spui, Haringvliet, Hollandsch Diep   This area continues from no. 1805 and is also much frequented by British visitors.

1809 Nieuwe Waterweg, Nieuwe- en Oude Maas, Spui en Noord, Dordtsche Kil, Brielse Meer   This serves for entry via Hook of Holland; or for continuation of no. 1807 to the Brielse Meer, Rotterdam, Dordrecht and the start of the inland route to Amsterdam.

1810 IJsselmeer met Randmeren   The IJsselmeer region and its entry points.

ANWB Charts

The chart series just mentioned serve most of the cruising grounds in this book. The remainder are covered by the ANWB *Waterkaarten;* folded maps of inland waterways which do not have English translations. Note that all dimensions on ANWB charts relating to depths and bridge clearances are given in decimetres (dm) instead of metres (1 metre = 10 dm). The most important abbreviations are: BB—opening bridge; H—bridge clearance (closed); and D—depth.

The map titles are prefixed by capital letters and the following ones complete the content of this book:

J   Grote Rivieren, westblad

H   Hollandse Plassen

G   Amsterdam—Alkmaar

F   Alkmaar—Den Helder (J–F cover the routes to Amsterdam)

B   Friese Meren (covers the Friesland lake district).

Tidal Atlases

The only rivers which are still open to the sea are those used for foreign trade: the West Schelde, leading to Flushing and Antwerp; and the River Maas, leading to Europoort and Rotterdam. The East Schelde is still tidal but has a flood barrier which, like the Thames barrier, is normally open. The south-west coast of the Netherlands is divided into islands by a large delta, where the Rhine, Maas and Schelde rivers converge to reach the sea. This is responsible for the complexity of the tidal streams and it is surprising how far inland their effects are felt. Although the cruising grounds contain vast areas of tideless waters, many tidal stretches remain and it is well worth having a tidal atlas for the waters you are cruising. The Dutch Hydrographic Service produce them in a similar format to their yachting charts. Atlases for the sailing areas in this book are:

a Stroomatlas Westerschelde   This covers the West Schelde from Flushing to Antwerp and corresponds to chart 1803, but also includes the coastal passage from Ostend to the Schelde.

c Stroomatlas Oosterschelde   Corresponds to chart 1805.

d Stroomatlas Benedenrivieren   Corresponds to chart 1809.

Information Services

The Netherlands Board of Tourism, 25–28 Buckingham Gate, London SW1E 6LD, tel (01) 630 0451 can supply much useful literature for the planning of your summer cruise.

On arrival in the Netherlands, the first place to aim for in each town is the local tourist information office. Called the vvv, it is always prominently signposted. Addresses for bicycle hire are given by the vvv but you must remember to take a passport when hiring. You may also need a passport in banks when obtaining cash with traveller's cheques, Eurocheques or credit cards.

Most large towns also have an office of the ANWB, the Dutch Touring Association which produces the *Almanak voor Watertoerisme* and the inland waterway charts already described. They are all sold at these offices together with the yacht chart books. But most important of all, they also supply a free leaflet of opening times for all the railway bridges in the Netherlands. As this is the only piece of essential information which is omitted from the Almanak, a visit to the first available office is advised.

Bridges

The majority of bridges in the Netherlands are too low for yachts with a fixed mast, but most can open (chart symbol **BB**) to allow such passage. On the busiest waterways bridges are much higher and passage may be possible without opening, depending on heights of mast and tide. Heights of bridges above mean HW (GHW) are given on charts and in the Almanak. Thus the most important thing to know is the exact metric height of your masthead above the waterline (or air draft). Guesswork is not good enough as a high tide may prevent a passage which is perfectly safe at low or half tide. All bridges over tidal waters exhibit vertical clearance gauges which allow a decision to be made on whether to proceed under the fixed part or await opening. Some bridge keepers have VHF radio and will give the exact clearance, or next opening time, on request.

The next important thing about bridges and locks is to know their opening times, given (in local time) in the Almanak and, for railway bridges, in the ANWB leaflet. The busiest road bridges only open at fixed times and the same applies to all railway bridges. The remainder open on approach and it is rarely

Fig. 2   Bridges

Hefbrug: as seen on route to Amsterdam between Gouda and Alphen (Chapter 9).

Ophaalbrug: drawbridge seen throughout the Netherlands. It may have double span.

*Basculebrug:
bascule bridge
seen throughout
the Netherlands.
Some have double
span.*

*Draaibrug: this
one is the
Stationsbrug swing
bridge at
Middelburg
(Chapter 4).*

*Pontonbrug or
vlotbrug: pontoon
bridge, as seen on
Noordollands
Kanaal between
Den Helder and
Alkmaar (Chapter
9).*

15

necessary to signal them; but if, during operating hours, you need to request opening, Morse **K** (– · –) is the sound signal to use. If you drop your foghorn overboard, or are otherwise unable to make sound signals, put the kettle on instead. This works like a charm for opening bridges. Nevertheless it can be very frustrating indeed to arrive at a bridge and discover, after a long wait, that it only opens twice a day or is closed on Sundays. However, this can all be avoided by checking the times beforehand. Light signals denote whether bridges and locks are closed, open, or about to open (explained in the next section on locks), but you can often hear when opening is imminent as bells ring when the road traffic barriers come down.

The names given to the different types of opening bridge are usually mentioned in the Almanak and it is worth knowing them as it makes a useful navigational check. The general term for any type of opening bridge is *beweegbare brug*. The different types and their Almanak abbreviations are as follows *(fig. 2)*.

Basculebrug (basc.): bascule bridge, usually with a single span but may have two (e.g. London's Tower Bridge).

Ophaalbrug (oph.): the typical 'Dutch bridge' or drawbridge.

Hefbrug (hef.): rising bridge; its span rises horizontally between two towers.

Draaibrug: swing bridge.

Pontonbrug, Vlotbrug: floating bridges, consisting of two floating sections which are drawn apart to open.

Locks

Yachtsmen making their first cruise to the Netherlands may be apprehensive, or blissfully ignorant, of the procedure to adopt when reaching a lock. First and foremost, remember that commercial traffic has precedence over pleasure craft. Don't rush in to the lock as soon as the gates start opening—another vessel may be coming out! Wait for the green traffic lights and give way to commercial craft. If in doubt, follow the Dutch yachts—not the Germans or Belgians, who might also be there for the first time.

Apart from a few places, there is no entry charge for bridges and locks; and they are all mechanically operated by highly efficient professional keepers. At the height of the holiday season a lock may be so full of craft as to make a sardine canner envious. At such times the lock keepers may broadcast instructions to proceed to a certain corner of the lock, so follow the other boats if you are not fluent in Dutch.

Arrival

As you approach the lock get fore-and-aft mooring lines and boathooks ready, and put fenders out on both sides. If the traffic light is green, you may enter. If there are two vertical lights, red over green, stand by: the lock will soon be ready for entry. If there is a single red light, wait. Two red vertical lights mean no passage possible; this signal is shown outside the normal opening hours. **All these light signals apply equally to bridges.**

If the red light is on, you may have to wait for some time before the standby signal is shown. In such cases you will save fuel by using the mooring facilities provided. There may be special provision for yachts such as a pontoon; or a mooring stage with posts which are close enough together and small enough

Fig. 3 Mooring
to barge post

for easy application of bow and stern lines. Alternatively there may only be a line of enormous barge posts which are too far apart to lie between. In that case, the simplest method is to gently approach a post on the windward side of the waterway and take a single line from your bow round a bollard on the leeward side of the post, and straight back to the bow cleat. The safest and most effective way of getting the line round a bollard is by looping it round the end of a boathook *(fig. 3)*. This gives extra reach and control and prevents losing the pulpit navigation light by collision with the post. Once secured by the bow the yacht will lie head to wind at a safe distance from the post.

Entry

When the red and green standby signal appears, start the engine but do not cast off your mooring lines. Traffic may still be coming out of the lock, and impatient yachtsmen may be motoring around the entrance in grave danger of collision with other vessels coming or going. As soon as the green entry light comes on, cast off and proceed cautiously into the lock, behind any commercial craft. The first task is to reduce speed until you have just sufficient steerage way for manoeuvrability, yet are not too close to the vessel ahead, which may suddenly run her engine full astern for no apparent reason. The next step is to tie up neatly to the side of the lock, which may not be as easy as it sounds, for with so many propellers churning up the water in a confined space, some quite unforeseen effects can occur, such as finding yourself moored at right angles to the length of the lock by your bow or stern. To avoid that embarrassment, ensure that crew at the bow and stern have lines and

17

boathooks ready. A line looped round the end of a boathook, as already described, is the easiest way of attaching to a bollard.

Once alongside, ensure that bow and stern lines are brought straight back on board and are in no way knotted round the bollard, ring, ladder step, or whatever else was used. Observing the high water level, shown by the weed on the lock walls, should indicate whether the boats are going to rise or fall. If falling, redeploy your lines to the lower attachment points on the wall and vice versa. But whatever you are attached by, make sure that your lines run free enough to be slackened off or hauled in easily as the water level changes. It may seem superfluous to add that bow or stern lines should *never* be secured to your deck cleats while the level is changing, but one has seen boats suspended in mid-air above a falling level until cleat parted company with deck and the boat returned to its natural environment. Always hold your mooring lines by hand and never secure them to a cleat. The prudent skipper will always have a hacksaw close at hand in case somebody forgets this golden rule.

Departure

Don't rush out as soon as the gates open. Although traffic from the lock has priority over craft waiting outside, you must wait for the green light and again give precedence to commercial craft. Furthermore, some locks have a road bridge over the gates and vessels without masts can leave before it is raised. Again it may seem superfluous to warn readers to wait for the bridge, but some yachts have lost expensive masthead equipment in their anxiety to leave as soon as the gates open.

If this account quenches your desire to visit the Netherlands, cast all fears aside and go. It only refers to your first experience and will not be nearly so bad as you imagine. After a few days you will become quite proficient at bridges and locks, and when you go again next time it all comes easily and naturally. But if, despite this reassurance, you still have forebodings about locks, there is a very simple way of overcoming them. Just enter the lock last of all and tie up alongside another yacht. Have plenty of fenders attached and choose a Dutch yacht. They all speak English, are far friendlier than anyone else, and know exactly what to do with your lines. Moreover, they can proffer expert advice on the best places to visit for the next part of your cruise.

Marinas

Most marinas *(jachthavens)* in the Netherlands are better, cleaner and cheaper than those in the UK. On arrival, make for the visitors' berth, which may be labelled:

Bezoekers; Passanten	visitors
Bezoekers hier melden	visitors report here
Bezoekers melden bij havenmeester	visitors report to Harbourmaster

Unoccupied moorings labelled *Vrij* (free) are available to visiting boats. Vacant berths which are labelled *Bezet* (occupied) must not be taken. In tidal waters boats are usually moored to pontoon finger berths. In non-tidal waters the commonest system is bow to landing stage, stern to posts. The Dutch term for this type of berth is *box (fig. 4)*. Mooring in a box can present some difficulty if you are short-handed and unaccustomed to the system, but it is

Fig. 4   Box Moorings

quite simple once you know how. Make up two stern lines of *floating* rope (polypropylene) and splice a 12 in.-diameter loop at one end, and a small one at the other end to fit your stern cleat. The line should be just longer than half the boat's length. For a crew of just skipper and mate, the procedure for berthing in a box is as follows.

1. Skipper stays at helm and engine controls.
2. Mate attaches stern line to stern cleat on windward side and leads rest of line forward outside rigging to widest part of boat.
3. Mate waits there with the loop as boat enters box, drops it over the upwind post as boat passes, and lets the rest of the line fall in the water.
4. Mate then proceeds immediately to bow to fend off and attach bow lines to landing stage. As the stern line floats there is no danger of fouling the propeller.
5. Skipper may now switch off engine, attach the leeward stern line and take in the slack from both stern lines.

Almost all marinas have shaver points and showers *(douches)* in the toilet blocks; but it is usually necessary to operate a slot machine for a hot shower. Coin boxes usually take a guilder coin (f1) or a token obtainable from the

Harbourmaster. Marinas or towns with launderettes *(wassalons)* are listed in the Index and the Almanak.

Drinking water is almost always available from a hose; while the larger marinas and most harbours have fuel pontoons which obviate any need to carry heavy cans of fuel or water from shore. Many marinas have 220 V electricity supply outlets and appliances which can be used from UK marina outlets will work satisfactorily; but a Continental plug, obtainable from local chandleries, is necessary. It is well worth taking a trickle charger to keep your batteries fully charged when staying in such marinas.

Food and Bottled Gas

Eating out is expensive, but fresh food can be bought at prices which are only slightly higher than at home. A full range of goods is usually obtainable at the local supermarket *(supermarkt)*. Remember that food shops are closed on Sundays and public holidays; and virtually all shops, including banks, close for an hour at lunchtime. Most shops and banks operate a ticket system to ensure that customers are served in turn. Take a ticket from the dispensing machine and sit down while waiting your turn, shown when your ticket number appears on the indicator.

Some useful words are:

aardappel	potato
bakker	baker
boter (gezouten)	butter (salted)
brood (gesneden)	bread (sliced)
eieren	eggs
groenten	vegetables
kaas	cheese
kip	chicken
melk	milk
—*half volle*	—half cream
—*koffie*	—evaporated
—*magere*	—skimmed
—*volle*	—full cream
spek	bacon
suiker	sugar
vis	fish
vlees	meat
vrucht	fruit

While most boats carry sufficient gas for a Netherlands holiday, those on extended cruises may well not have enough. As Calor gas is not used on the Continent there are very few places where such bottles can be replaced or refilled. It would accordingly be worthwhile taking a Camping Gaz adaptor, obtainable from chandleries in Britain, which permits the use of Camping Gaz bottles which are available throughout both Europe and the UK.

Medical Treatment

The Netherlands is an EEC country and British visitors are accordingly eligible for treatment on the same terms as Dutch nationals. Free hospital and medical treatment is provided but prescriptions and dental treatment must be paid for. However, these benefits are not available unless you already have a certificate of entitlement, form E111 obtainable on application to your local office of the Department of Health & Social Security, which also issues a leaflet explaining the procedure involved. Some useful Dutch words are: *arts*—doctor; *apotheek* or *drogisterij*—chemist's shop; *ziekenhuis*—hospital; *tandarts*—dentist.

Time

Dutch local time is GMT + 1 in winter and GMT + 2 in summer. Opening times in the Almanak for bridges and locks are local time; but the tide tables are GMT + 1, which is the same as British Summer Time. All times in this book are Dutch local time.

Day Signals and Lights

Finally, readers are reminded that the Collision Regulations are international: they apply just as much in the waterways of the Netherlands as they do in the open sea. This is particularly important in the case of vessels at anchor or motor-sailing, where the required signals are not often seen on British yachts. In the Netherlands these signals *must* be used, and any omissions may well lead to a visit from the marine police.

At anchor in daylight a black ball must be hoisted; and at night an all-round white light must be shown. When motor-sailing in daylight a black cone, point down, must be raised forward; at night the correct lights for a vessel under power must be shown. A masthead trilight may only be used when sailing, not when motor-sailing.

Night sailing in inland waters will depend on whether bridges and locks are open after dark. This information is given throughout the text, and in the Almanak. Where night passages are possible, the waterways are well marked with light buoys, beacons and leading lights.

CHAPTER 2

The Delta Project

The parts of the Netherlands most frequently visited by British yachts are the provinces of Zeeland and South Holland, conveniently entered via Flushing. They are the nearest to our east and south coasts, and for anything up to a three week holiday they form the limit of what can comfortably be covered on a family cruise. The Delta Project has transformed this area from a complex system of tideways and islands into an unrivalled expanse of non-tidal lakes and sheltered waterways. Before describing the cruising grounds this chapter will explain how that transformation came about.

Between Flushing and Hook of Holland, the Netherlands coast is a delta formed by the rivers Rhine, Maas and Schelde as they reach the North Sea. The coastline is a complex of islands and waterways and it can be quite difficult to grasp which waterway arises from which river. The land lies below sea level and for centuries has been protected by dykes. However, on the night of January 31–February 1, 1953 a ferocious north-westerly storm over the North Sea combined with a spring tide to produce some of the worst flooding ever experienced in the Netherlands. The dykes were breached in 89 places, 1,853 people drowned and enormous areas of land were inundated. Shocked by this disaster, the Dutch nation resolved that it should never happen again. The government accordingly implemented the Delta Project in 1958, with the aim of sealing the seaward entrances to this part of the Netherlands. The only seaways to be left open were those used for foreign trade: the West Schelde, leading to Flushing and Antwerp; and the New Waterway leading from Hook of Holland and Europoort to Rotterdam. *Fig. 5* shows the delta as it was in the 18th century, and *fig. 6* after completion of the Delta Project in 1987.

In 1958, at Krimpen aan de IJssel, a flood barrier across the Hollandsche IJssel was completed. This protects the lowest part of the Netherlands, an area north and east of Rotterdam that is 6 metres below sea level and has a population of two million. The Krimpen barrier is on the inland route to Amsterdam and is described in Chapter 9. In 1960 the Zandkreek channel between South and North Beveland was dammed. Its seaward end, the Veerse Gat between Walcheren and North Beveland which led to the port of Veere, was dammed in 1961 to create a tideless salt water lake called the Veerse Meer (Chapter 4). By 1965 the Grevelingen channel between Duiveland and Overflakkee was dammed at Bruinisse. Its seaward end, the Brouwershavense Gat, was closed between Schouwen and Goeree in 1972 to form another tideless saline lake called the Grevelingenmeer (Chapter 6).

In 1971 the Haringvliet estuary was closed off from the North Sea by

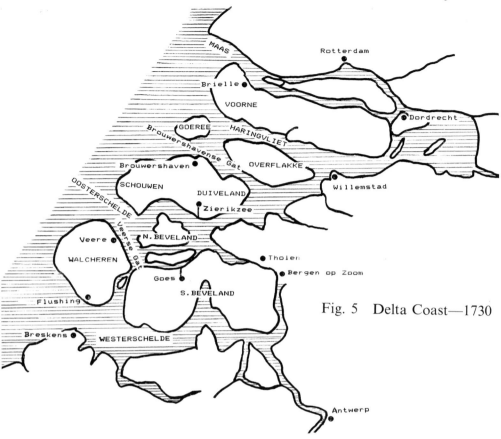

Fig. 5 Delta Coast—1730

construction of the Haringvlietdam between Goeree and Voorne. Its inland
end was closed in the same year, transforming the Haringvliet into a tideless
fresh water lake open only to the Hollandsch Diep. This closure was effected
by the Volkerakdam which connects Overflakkee and North Brabant. It
sealed off the fresh water of the Haringvliet and Hollandsch Diep from the
Volkerak tideway which originated from the East Schelde. This area is
described in Chapter 7. By 1972 the Delta Project had shortened the coastline
by over 400 miles and tamed the flooding power of the sea. By creating three
non-tidal lakes—the Veerse Meer, Grevelingenmeer and Haringvliet—it
endowed the Netherlands with a superb expanse of sheltered sailing waters.
But it has also provided a system of water control which can deal not only with
any threat from seaward, but also with flood waters coming downstream from
the Rhine and Maas. The nerve centre of this control system is the
Haringvlietdam.

The River Rhine rises in Switzerland and makes its way along the Franco-
German border before entering the Netherlands as the Rijn. It then divides
into a northbound branch called the IJssel, which drains into the IJsselmeer,
and two westbound branches called the Lek and the Waal. Both of these
formerly reached the North Sea via Hook of Holland and the Haringvliet

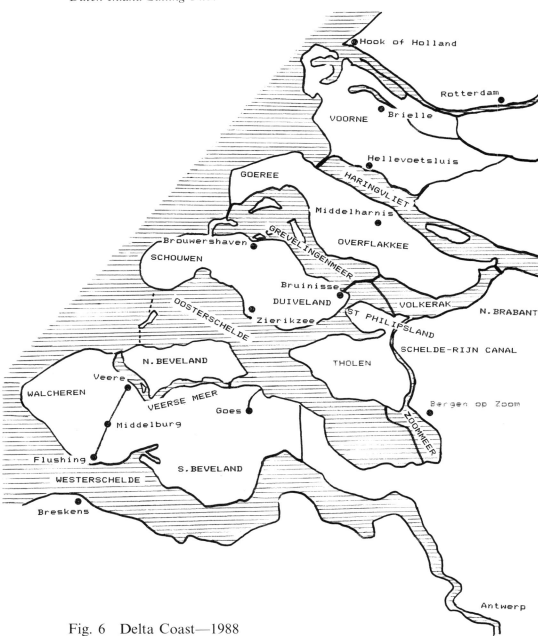

Fig. 6   Delta Coast—1988

estuary. The River Maas rises in France as the Meuse, flows through Belgium and enters the Netherlands as the Maas. Like the Rhine it formerly had an uninterrupted passage to the North Sea via Hook of Holland and the Haringvliet. The Delta Project has provided two routes for this seaward flow from the Rhine and Maas: direct into the North Sea via Hook of Holland; and into the Haringvliet lake where it is trapped by the Haringvlietdam, the sluices in which accordingly act as the stopcock of the western Netherlands. When river flow is minimal the sluices are closed to conserve fresh water; the Hook of Holland then becomes the only exit for fresh water, and this outward flow prevents water from the North Sea penetrating inland to contaminate the fresh water. When the river flow is maximal the dam sluices open at low tide, allowing excess fresh water to overflow into the North Sea. This prevents a buildup of the fresh water flow through Hook of Holland, which would create an adverse current for shipping bound for Rotterdam. Between these two extremes the Haringvlietdam sluices maintain correct water levels and supplies throughout the country. By controlling the outward flow of fresh water via Rotterdam and Hook of Holland they not only prevent this busiest of seaways from silting up, but also prevent saline contamination of fresh waters.

The next stage of the Delta Project was the closure of the East Schelde. Originally it was planned to seal off the river completely, but after much opposition from environmental and fishing interests a compromise solution was found: to build a flood barrier across the estuary from North Beveland to Schouwen. It was completed in 1987 and is similar to the Thames flood barrier insofar as it stays open and permits normal tidal flow but can be shut off from the North Sea if any flood danger arises. A lock allows passage between sea and river.

The final stages of the 30 year Delta Project were also completed in 1987. Two new dams, Philipsdam and Oesterdam, across the inland reaches of the East Schelde have created two non-tidal compartments within the East Schelde which effectively prevent any salt contamination of the Haringvliet and Hollandsch Diep. The Philipsdam, extending from St Philipsland to the Grevelingendam, turns the Volkerak into a tideless compartment between the Philipsdam and the Volkerakdam. At the southeast end of the East Schelde, the Oesterdam between South Beveland and Tholen has created another such compartment called the Zoommeer. This has transformed the Schelde-Rijn Canal and the harbours of Bergen op Zoom and Tholen into tideless areas. Access to the North Sea from the East Schelde is still possible through the Roompotsluis (lock), and from the Haringvliet through another lock called the Goereesesluis. Compartmentalization of the East Schelde still permits passage throughout its former tideways via locks in the dams: from the Veerse Meer through the Zandkreekdam; into the Grevelingenmeer through the Grevelingendam; into the Volkerak through the Philipsdam; into the Haringvliet and Hollandsch Diep through the Volkerakdam; and through the Oesterdam into the Zoommeer for Tholen and Bergen op Zoom.

The Delta Project has not only protected the land against flooding but has also provided the people with vast tracts of tideless water which are superb recreational areas. Furthermore the new non-tidal waterways are far safer for commercial craft too, while the motorways across the new dams have greatly improved road communications and shortened travelling times throughout the Netherlands. It is one of the world's greatest engineering feats, and the fascinating story is best appreciated by visiting the Haringvliet Expo at the Haringvlietdam, and the Delta Expo on the East Schelde flood barrier.

CHAPTER 3

West Schelde

Chart 1803
This series is entitled *Westerschelde, Vlissingen tot Antwerpen en Kanaal Van Terneuzen naar Gent*, which means West Schelde, Flushing to Antwerp, and the Terneuzen-Ghent Canal *(fig. 7)*. The first sheet (1803.1) is a passage planning chart and shows Flushing (Vlissingen) and Breskens on opposite sides of the mouth of the River Schelde. These are the commonest entry and departure points for most British yachts. Upriver, it shows how the West Schelde leads across the Belgian frontier to Antwerp; and how it connects with the East Schelde (Oosterschelde) directly between Hansweert and Wemeldinge via the Kanaal door Zuid Beveland; or indirectly via Flushing, Middelburg and Veere along the Kanaal door Walcheren into the Veerse Meer. It also shows the start of the canal from Terneuzen to the Belgian city of Ghent. (A visit to Antwerp is strongly recommended and the passage is well described in the books mentioned in Chapter 1.)

You can spend a pleasant holiday making a round trip from Flushing through the Kanaal door Walcheren to Middelburg and Veere. Then through the Veerse Meer into the East Schelde to visit Zierikzee and Goes, before returning to the West Schelde from Wemeldinge via the Kanaal door Zuid Beveland. Thence from Hansweert to Breskens to start the passage home.

The Zoommeer, a new lake created by the final stage of the Delta Project, contains the former East Schelde harbours of Bergen op Zoom and Tholen, and it may seem strange for these to be included in chart 1803. The reason for this anomaly is that the Zoommeer is now dammed off from the East Schelde and has become part of the course of the Schelde-Rijn Canal which starts from the West Schelde near Antwerp. But as Tholen and Bergen op Zoom are only accessible to yachts via the East Schelde, they will be described in Chapter 5.

Ostend to Flushing

This coastal passage is well shown in Dutch chart series 1801 of the North Sea coast. The two most important things to note about the West Schelde are the strength of its tides and the density of traffic. A passage from Ostend to Flushing can be made comfortably on one tide, and the huge cranes at Flushing are usually visible soon after passing Zeebrugge. It is essential to reach the Schelde before the tide turns, as it can run out of the estuary at 3 knots and greatly increase your fuel bill. Once past Zeebrugge, keep well

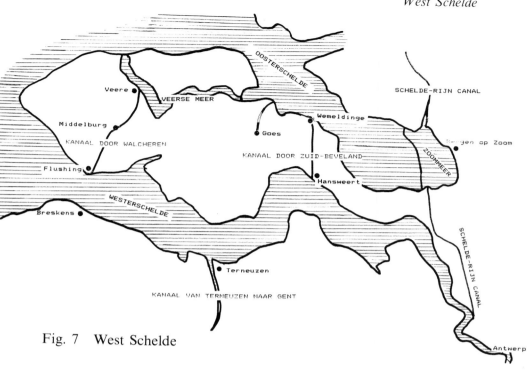

Fig. 7   West Schelde

inshore of the buoyed channel as there is enough depth to sail quite close to the shore. The most prominent landmark as you reach the Schelde is the black and white striped Nieuwe Sluis lighthouse. Once there, you can tell the tide direction from the shipping in the anchorage.

The way into Flushing is shown by the Breskens–Flushing ferries which cross continuously and are easily recognized by their symmetrical outlines. If unsure of the way, just follow one and it will lead you straight to Flushing lock and your entrance to the inland waterways. The ferry route is shown on charts 1801.2 and 1803.2. A traffic separation scheme is in force on the Flushing side of the river, where the channel runs surprisingly close inshore; it must be crossed at a right angle in compliance with Rule 10 of the Collision Regulations. The Schelde Information Service on VHF channel 14 broadcasts hourly in English (H + 50).

Chart 1803.2 *Vlissingen tot Terneuzen* (Flushing to Terneuzen) shows the way into Breskens, Flushing and Terneuzen; and the first part of a passage upriver to the Hansweert–Wemeldinge Canal, or to Antwerp itself.

Breskens

This town makes a very convenient first or last port of call in the Netherlands. Situated on the S bank of the Schelde entrance, Breskens is directly opposite Flushing and is accessible at all states of the tide. It has two important advantages over Flushing: no locks or bridges, and a very large, very good marina. It accordingly provides an excellent stopover while waiting for tide or

Westerschelde: the strength of tidal stream throughout this river is well shown by the spar buoy.

weather. The absence of locks and bridges ensures that departure plans are not disrupted by unexpected delays.

The harbour entrance is narrow, between two stone moles, and care must be taken to allow for the set of a very strong tide. Once through the entrance there is plenty of sheltered room for attending to sails, fenders and mooring lines, provided that the fishing or racing fleets are not passing through at the same time. As the chart inset shows, bear round to port for the marina (Jachthaven) and go straight to the reception pontoon at the N end, where one of the staff is usually waiting to direct you to a vacant berth.

Having reached the allotted berth, newcomers are often unable to puzzle out the mooring method. Boats are moored bow to a pontoon, and the puzzle is to find out where the stern line comes from. The answer is shown in the diagram *(fig. 8)*. The marina's stern line is attached to a ringbolt just above water level on the front of the pontoon facing the bow; it passes straight down to a mooring block on the bottom. Having secured the bow to the pontoon, pick up the stern line and take it aft to the stern. Then haul in the slack and attach it to the stern cleat. As the line is covered in weed and sharp barnacles, it is advisable to wear gloves. To depart, cast off the stern line and give it time to sink to the bottom before reversing from the pontoon. Also take care not to foul your propeller on the stern lines of boats opposite.

The clubhouse and restaurant, Harbourmaster, launderette and toilets are housed in one block. The facilities are some of the best in the Netherlands, with plenty of hot water, but the marina charges are above average. Water hoses and electricity on the pontoons, fuel from a barge on the E side of the fishing harbour (Oosthaven) next to the marina. The Harbourmaster will advise you where to clear Customs.

The Breskens ferry cruises Westerschelde between Breskens and Flushing. Follow this ferry to find Flushing lock.

Ashore

Harbour facilities at Breskens include chandleries, boatyard, sailmaker, Proctor mast depot, and freshly caught fried fish with chips. The harbour is separated from the town by a very high dyke. Although small, the town contains all the necessities—supermarket, shops, bank, restaurants and vvv office—but you have to penetrate the back streets to find them all. Half-day closing is Tuesday but the supermarket remains open. The local yacht club is on the main road beneath the dyke, opposite the harbour, and welcomes visitors.

Fig. 8   Breskens Marina

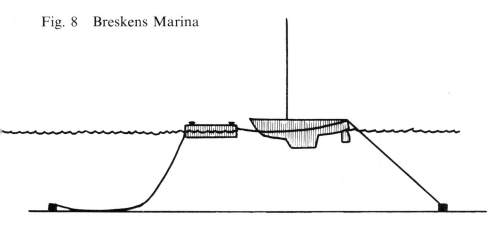

Flushing (Vlissingen)

Flushing and its approaches are shown on sheet 1803.2, but the port itself is shown on a larger scale on sheet 1803.8. 2.5 miles opposite Breskens, Flushing gives access through a lock to all the Dutch inland cruising grounds. Just follow the Breskens ferry to Flushing lock. Do not be misled by the yacht berth symbol in the old port of Flushing, shown on sheet 1803.8: this is in the Visserhaven which is entered through a lock gate but has not yet been developed as a yacht harbour. Pilot boats moor at the old port entrance. Access to the inland waters is through locks in the Buitenhaven, a mile upriver from the old port entrance. Ferries from Sheerness and Breskens, and much commercial traffic, make for the entrance to the Buitenhaven, which is marked by a small wooden pier.

Flushing Locks

After rounding the wooden pier, the locks will be seen to port, quite close to the Breskens ferry terminus *(Veersteiger)*. There is one large and one small lock, and yachts usually use the smaller. Customs officers may come on board at the lock. There are no special yacht mooring facilities outside the locks, but waiting time is short and there is enough space to keep out of the way of passing traffic. The locks open at all times and use VHF channel 22. Flushing port radio uses channel 14.

Once inside, with the gates closed, you get a wonderful feeling of relief at being sheltered from the rough and dangerous seas you traversed from home. On the other hand, you will experience a great sadness when the gates open on your way back from the placid waters of the Netherlands.

If this is your first Dutch port of call and Customs officers have not come aboard at the lock, you must contact them before proceeding. On leaving the lock, tie up to the wall and ask the lock keeper to direct you. The Customs office is only a few minutes' walk, on the E side of the station; it is shown on Dutch charts by a symbol resembling that for the London Underground.

Flushing Marina

Leaving the lock, go straight ahead until you see the top of Flushing bridge on your starboard bow. Continue in the direction of the bridge, and when it comes into full view the marina entrance will be seen on the starboard side. It is a very small marina with box moorings, but has a cosy clubhouse which serves good meals. There are coin-operated showers, water hoses and a diesel pump. It is only a short walk from the railway station and Sheerness ferry terminus.

It takes about half an hour to walk into town from the marina, but can be done as a circular trip: turn left at the marina exit but return via the riverside to the locks. Flushing has a good shopping centre and can provide a full range of services. There is a launderette at 15 Holbeinstraat.

Flushing Bridge (Keersluisbrug)

This is the first of five bridges across the Kanaal door Walcheren, which goes from Flushing to Middelburg and Veere. All can be called on VHF channel 22 and their opening times are: Mon–Sat 06–22h; Sun and hols 07–11,

Terneuzen: entrance to Veerhaven from Westerschelde yacht mooring pontoons of WV De Honte, WV Neusen off photo to right.

17–21h. As the Keersluisbrug serves the railway station some waiting is inevitable, especially during rush hours. There are no yacht moorings on the seaward side of the bridge but one can usually tie up alongside another vessel. Places where mooring is forbidden may show various signs, such as *Verboden te Meren, Aanleggen Verboden, Geen Ligplaats,* or *Prive.* Passage along the canal from Flushing to Middelburg and Veere is described in the next chapter as it extends into chart 1805. Although it is only 3 miles to Middelburg it takes an hour or two, depending on the bridge openings; but it has a much better, bigger and pleasantly situated marina in a far nicer town. For this reason most yachts proceed straight from the lock to Middelburg without stopping at Flushing.

Terneuzen

This is the seaward end of the canal to Ghent (Kanaal van Terneuzen naar Gent), where the French and Belgian canal systems merge with the Dutch. It is possible to get from Terneuzen to Ghent with a fixed mast, but beyond there, whether going to Calais, Brussels or Paris, masts must be lowered. The Belgian city of Ghent is about 18 miles from Terneuzen and well worth visiting, being rather like Bruges in many respects though larger and more varied. Charts 1803.6 and 7 cover the route from Terneuzen to Ghent.

As the 1803.2 chart inset and Almanak show, the yacht harbour is in the Veerhaven, which is the easternmost of three entrances from the Westerschelde. The westernmost (Westbuitenhaven) has an enormous lock for ocean-going vessels; and is forbidden to yachts. The middle entrance (Oostbuitenhaven) is the one to enter if you wish to proceed up the canal to

Ghent; but if bound for the yacht harbour only, enter the Veerhaven and make for the pontoon moorings at the S end. These comprise two marinas: the westernmost being that of the Royal Belgian Sailing Club and W.V. De Honte; the other belongs to the W.V. Neusen. The former marina is usually crowded but the Harbourmaster is very helpful and packs in visiting yachts like sardines in a can. The toilet block has free showers and a small launderette (tokens from HM), a drier and telephone. The pontoons have free water and electricity. The W.V. Neusen has similar facilities but no launderette.

There is a good shopping precinct just five minutes from the harbour and some fine walks along the dyke with good views of the river and canal traffic. The town itself has little of the usual Dutch charm or appeal. If bound for Ghent there is a marina in the canal itself. After passing through the lock (Oostsluis) in the Oostbuitenhaven, take the hairpin bend to port and enter Zijkanaal A where the marina will be found at its northern end.

Charts 1803.3, *Terneuzen tot Bath*, and 1803.2 cover the passage from Breskens or Flushing to Terneuzen and Hansweert. This is the entrance to the Hansweert–Wemeldinge Canal (Kanaal door Zuid-Beveland) which is a useful and worthwhile short-cut to the East Schelde. This canal will be described in Chapter 5 as it is covered by chart series 1805.

The most important aspect of a passage to Terneuzen or Hansweert is to get the tide right. It is 11 miles from Flushing or Breskens to Terneuzen, and 20 to Hansweert. The tide is fair from Flushing HW − 5 to HW + 1. (Flushing tide tables are given in British and Dutch almanacs.) If you possess the Dutch tidal atlas of the West Schelde—which is strongly recommended—you will see that the tide runs at over 3 knots, so there is plenty of time available to complete the passage. In fact, one can sail all the way to Antwerp on one tide. From Flushing or Breskens, stay on that side of the river and keep a good lookout for the very heavy traffic, especially off Terneuzen where the Belgian canal system joins the Schelde.

Hansweert

Those who have not entered Hansweert recently will find some changes. Instead of three locks there is now only one, the Oostsluis, to be replaced in 1988 by a new one farther N. There are no special yacht berths or moorings for waiting, but one can lie to one of the barge mooring stages. The lock opens at all times and listens on VHF channel 22.

CHAPTER 4

Flushing to Veerse Meer

Charts 1803, 1805

The Kanaal door Walcheren goes from Flushing to Middelburg, and then to Veere where it enters a lake called the Veerse Meer. The passage from Flushing to Middelburg is on chart 1803.8, while chart 1805 covers the rest of the canal, the Veerse Meer and also the East Schelde and Grevelingenmeer *(fig. 9)*.

The Kanaal door Walcheren connects the West Schelde and the Veerse Meer and has a lock at each end. As on all waterways, keep to the starboard side and give way to commercial craft. (The first lock at Flushing was described in Chapter 3.) The only stopping place along the canal is Middelburg, halfway between Flushing and Veere. It is a lovely place and should not be missed. It is 3 miles and five bridges from Flushing.

All five bridges listen on VHF channel 22 and open: Mon–Sat 06–22h; Sun and hols 07–11, 17–21h. All have mooring stages, except the seaward side of Flushing bridge. From seaward, they are:

1. Flushing bridge (Chapter 3): an *ophaalbrug* called the Keersluisbrug
2. Sloebrug: *ophaalbrug* opens on approach
3. Souburg swing bridge: opens on approach
4. Middelburg (Schroebrug): *ophaalbrug*
5. Middelburg (Stationsbrug): swing bridge to railway station.

Bridges 1, 4, 5, carry heavy traffic, while 1 and 5 serve railway stations. There may well be a wait of half an hour or so before these bridges can open, especially during rush hours, so make use of the mooring stages, or put the kettle on!

Middelburg

Mooring to the canal wall in Middelburg is forbidden; if you wish to stop proceed to the yacht harbour. The entrance is E of the swing bridge (Stationsbrug) on the N bank of the canal (1803.8) and is indicated by a Jachthaven sign. As you enter the inlet there is a fuel barge on your port side. Carry on past the box moorings until you see the Harbourmaster's office and reception stage in front of you. If you wish to stay overnight, proceed to the reception stage, otherwise go to the short stay (2 hours only) landing stage opposite. Middelburg is a far better shopping centre than Veere so it is worth stocking up with supplies here.

Fig. 9   East Schelde

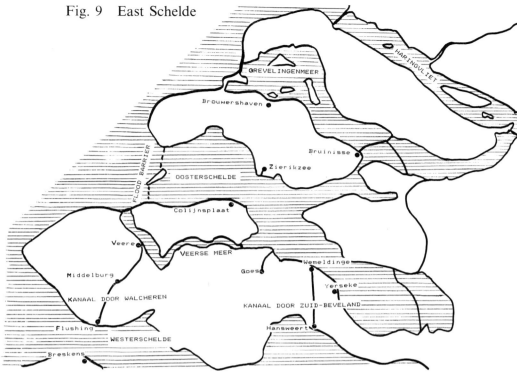

If staying overnight, the Harbourmaster will allocate one of the box moorings already passed or one beyond the harbour bridge. This attractive bascule bridge (Spijkerbrug) next to the office opens daily on the half hour, 0930–2130. There are electricity points and water hoses on the landing stages.

The clubhouse (W.V. Arne) is situated on the opposite side of the bridge from the office, just past a chandlery. It was formerly an East India Company warehouse. Washrooms, showers (coins), toilets and a launderette (tokens) occupy the ground floor. The bar upstairs is open until midnight.

Capital of the province of Zeeland, Middelburg dates back to 1103. It was devastated by bombing in 1940 and has been rebuilt in the original style. There are many magnificent buildings, particularly the 1452 Stadhuis and 1123 Toren 'Lange Jan' which is 88 m high. The panoramic view of Walcheren from the top of the tower is reward enough for the climb. Another great attraction is the 1:20 scale model of Walcheren (Miniatuur Walcheren) set in a park.

The town is an excellent shopping centre. Half-day closing is Monday and market day Thursday. There is a chandlery, boatyard and sailmaker. The vvv office is in the market square and the ANWB office is at 26 Lange Geere. Bicycles can be hired from the railway station, but don't forget your passport. Apart from the shopping precincts in the town centre there is an enormous supermarket just five minutes' walk from the market square, or ten minutes from the yacht harbour. It has a bank where all currencies are handled and Eurocheques can be cashed. Between the yacht harbour and the supermarket there is a superb new public library (*openbaare bibliotheek*) where you can read

Middelburg: short stay landing stage. Up to two hours allowed. Water available from a hose at harbourmaster's office opposite.

up-to-date English newspapers; and borrow books for up to three months if you can produce a British public library ticket.

Middelburg to Veere (chart 1805.2)

Departing from Middelburg, past the fuel barge, watch out for through traffic before turning to port for the 3 mile stretch to Veere lock. As there are no bridges it is possible to run all the way under sail if the wind is fair. The first 2 miles are straight and you can put this to good advantage by checking your steering compass against the chart direction. Furthermore, there are kilometre posts on the E bank, so you can also check the accuracy of your log and speed readings (1 km = 0.54 n. miles). Looking astern, there is a beautiful silhouette of Middelburg; and to each side you may see cows grazing the banks while oystercatchers, greenshanks and wagtails patrol the water's edge. Then, as you approach a bend in the canal, you see the lovely tower at Veere on the port bow. On rounding the bend Veere lock is straight ahead.

There are mooring stages and plenty of room to manoeuvre if the two locks are closed on arrival. The E lock is the larger and the one usually used. They listen on VHF channel 22 and open Mon–Sat 05–23.30h; Sun and hols 05–23h.

Veere: entrance to Kanaal door Walcheren from Veerse Meer, showing Veere locks and canal leading towards Middelburg and Flushing.

Veere

From Veere lock a short final stretch of the Walcheren Canal has a boatyard and small marina on its W side before it joins the Veerse Meer. Veere is on the same side, at the entrance to the Meer. Turn left on entering, outside the withies, and moor at the short stay landing stage if you are not staying overnight. The harbour just beyond has a very narrow entrance, and care must be taken to avoid vessels leaving. If you wish to stay overnight in Veere, enter the harbour and go alongside the landing stage on the port side. However, Veere is so popular that you will most likely find it full and have to tie up alongside a trot of visiting yachts, but at busy times the Harbourmaster will probably be directing visitors to berths. The mooring boxes are all reserved for local boats. The office and clubhouse are in the building above the landing stage. Apart from the bar, there are toilet and washing facilities with coin operated showers. Water is from hoses.

Before the great flood disaster of 1953, Veere was a fishing port on the Veerse Gat which led directly from the North Sea. Completion of the Veersedam in 1961 closed off the Veerse Gat from the sea and created a tideless salt water lake called the Veerse Meer. A flourishing port in the Middle Ages, specializing in the wool trade with Scotland, Veere is no longer a seaport but has become one of the most popular water sports centres in the Netherlands. The entrance to the harbour is dominated by the Campveerse tower and cannons on the ramparts. The town itself is quite small but it has a fine 1474 town hall with an outstanding belfry tower. This, together with the Campveerse tower and domed Grote Kerk, gives Veere its distinctive skyline. In 1811 Napoleon commandeered the Grote Kerk for use as a military hospital.

There are not many shops but all the essentials are available and close at hand, including a chandlery. Along the narrow cobbled streets are all the

Veere: entrance to Veere harbour from Veerse Meer. Short stay landing stage at left of picture. Left to right: Groute Kerk, Campveerse Tower, Town Hall Belfry.

shops and a pottery where you can watch the potters at work. Across the bridge over the inner harbour is a small toilet block with showers (coins), and beyond that a walk along the town wall brings you to a windmill.

The Veerse Meer

For many British yachtsmen the Veerse Meer provides their first experience of a sheltered, tideless cruising ground. It makes a welcome change from home waters or the continental coast, where each passage between harbours can be an uncomfortable battle with the elements. Catering for all types of water sport, the Veerse Meer contains excellent marinas for those who want all the facilities they offer; and many small islands for those who prefer more natural surroundings (charts 1805.2 and 3).

The direction of buoyage is from the Zandreekdam to the Veersedam. Depths range from 3.5 m to 25 m in the well lit, buoyed and beaconed channels. The 1.5 m contour is marked by port and starboard withies. As there are no tides, go aground gently if you must.

Sealed off from the sea by the Veersedam at its N end, the Veerse Meer is 12 miles long *(fig. 10)*. Its E end is sealed off from the East Schelde by the Zandkreekdam between North and South Beveland, but a lock gives access to the East Schelde and all the cruising grounds beyond.

Veersedam

The Veersedam which separates the Meer from the North Sea is well worth visiting and just a short sail from Veere, past the windmill and Oostwatering marina on the W side. It is possible to moor at the base of the dam. Go ashore and ascend the steps to the top where you will see the sand dunes and sea below, the East Schelde flood barrier to the E, and fine views of the Veerse

Meer and Walcheren to the S and W. In a northerly blow, the view of the North Sea will induce a satisfying feeling of relief at being on the right side of the dam. There is a restaurant and shop at the base of the dam where you can get hot take-away meals or barbecue dishes ready for cooking.

Oostwatering Marina

The entrance to this marina is $\frac{3}{4}$ mile NW of Veere. Visiting yachts moor to finger berths. There are fuel pumps, full boatyard repair facilities, a chandlery, food shop, restaurant, showers (coins) and a launderette (tokens and washing powder from the chandlery).

Kamperland

On the other side of the lake, directly opposite Veere, a short length of canal leads to the village of Kamperland. There is a small marina at the canal entrance with showers and a diesel pump. The end of the canal has a mooring stage which is convenient for shopping in the village.

Islands

One of the great attractions of the Veerse Meer is its abundance of islands where you can stop overnight, free of charge, at proper mooring stages. They are all uninhabited but are kept clean and tidy, with refuse disposal bins, flush toilets and well equipped barbecue sites. They offer a pleasant alternative to the noise and night life of a harbour; without the glare of streetlights you can observe the stars, enjoy the solitude, listen to the wildlife and picnic in lovely wooded surroundings. Most of the islands have more than one mooring site so you can usually choose one on the leeward side.

Returning from the Veersedam along the opposite side from Veere, you pass the islands of Schutteplaat, Mosselplaat, Haringvreter and Arneplaat, all of which are less than 2 miles from Veere and very convenient night stops if the harbour is full. Haringvreter is the largest island in the Veerse Meer and the only one with four-legged animals—cattle, sheep, horses, deer and lots of rabbits. Walking through the woods you can see game birds, and at the marshy S end there are flocks of swans, gulls and waders, including avocets, godwits, oystercatchers, curlews and redshanks. On one quiet night the author watched a seal beach itself opposite his boat.

Continuing onto chart 1805.3, there are more picnic sites and night stops on the islands of Bastiaan de Langeplaat, Spieringplaat, Zandkreekplaat, Schelphoekplaat and Sabbingeplaat. Just past these last two islands, and 2 miles from the Zandkreekdam, there are two large marinas at Kortgene on the N bank and Wolphaartsdijk on the S. Both provide all facilities and are convenient for refuelling.

Zandkreek Lock

The Zandkreeksluis affords passage through the Zandkreekdam between the Veerse Meer and East Schelde. It opens at all hours and uses VHF channel 18. There are yacht mooring pontoons at both ends, toilets and refuse bins near the control tower. As the East Schelde is tidal, there can be a considerable rise

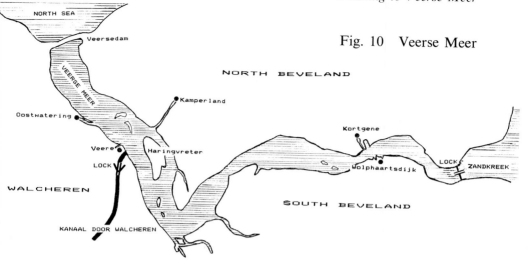

Fig. 10   Veerse Meer

or fall of water level while in the lock, so make sure your warps are free to run; and wait for the bridge across the end of the lock to open before rushing out. If, having arrived at the lock, you wish to stop overnight, there are mooring stages in the Veerse Meer at the S end of the Zandkreekdam, where you will be sheltered from the wash of passing traffic, but the depth is under 2 m.

CHAPTER 5

East Schelde

Chart 1805

An overall picture of the waterways of Zeeland and South Holland is shown on chart 1805.1. The previous chapter described access to the East Schelde (Oosterschelde) via the Veerse Meer and Zandkreek lock, a route shown on charts 1805.2 and 3. Series 1805 also shows access from the North Sea through the Roompot lock (Roompotsluis) in the new flood barrier; the direct access from the West Schelde through the Hansweert–Wemeldinge Canal (Kanaal door Zuid-Beveland); and the two new dams, Philipsdam and Oesterdam. The East Schelde cruising ground *(fig. 11)* contains the harbours of Burghsluis, Colijnsplaat, Zierikzee, Goes, Yerseke, Tholen and Bergen op Zoom, all of which are described in this chapter; but the Grevelingenmeer, which is now included in chart 1805, is covered in the next chapter.

A glance at any of the charts of the Oosterschelde tideways will be sufficient to show the sandbanks and choice of buoyed channels which are typical of this river. While this will be quite straightforward for bilge-keeled yachts accustomed to the Thames estuary, those unsuited to take the ground should be careful not to stray from buoyed channels. The final stages of the Delta Project have wrought great changes in this cruising ground and up-to-date charts are essential. Without them, yachtsmen who last sailed this area in 1986 may well feel lost, and should discard any chart editions dated 1986 or earlier.

Chart 1805.8 *Oosterscheldekering tot Zeelandbrug* (East Schelde Barrier to Zeeland Bridge) covers the North Sea entrance to the Oosterschelde through the flood barrier lock, together with the harbours of Burghsluis, Colijnsplaat and Zierikzee. The flood barrier is similar to the Thames barrier insofar as it is only closed when flooding is imminent. Thus the river remains tidal and use of the Dutch tidal atlas *(Stroomatlas Oosterschelde)* is recommended: it is based on LW Zierikzee, but gives equivalent times based on HW Flushing.

Oosterschelde Flood Barrier

The Dutch name for the East Schelde flood barrier is Stormvloedkering, which translates as storm-surge barrier. Ceremonially opened in 1987, it is one of the showpieces of the Delta Project. The first stages of this great engineering feat were the construction of two artificial work islands on the Roggenplaat and Neeltje Jans sandbanks. These reduced the mouth of the river from one wide opening to three small ones; and the flood barrier accordingly consists of three sections across these openings. Piers support guillotine gates which are

Fig. 11   East Schelde
Cruising Area

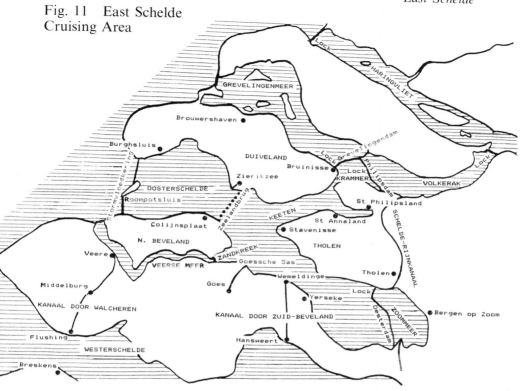

kept raised to allow normal tidal flow, but can be lowered to seal off the river from the North Sea. The new islands were used as construction sites for the barrier components. A motorway is now being built across the top of the storm-surge barrier.

The history of the Delta Project and the Stormvloedkering is displayed in a magnificent exhibition called Delta Expo which is housed on the island of Neeltje Jans. The entrance fee includes the exhibition building, with a superb view from the top, a boat trip along the barrier and a visit to one of the barrier gates. The power and speed of the tide surging through is a sight which may impress or frighten; but it is not surprising, since the former wide-open river mouth has now been reduced to three open channels which are together less than half the original width.

Access to the exhibition is solely by special bus from the ticket office at the N end of the barrier. There is a bus service to this point from Zierikzee, but it can also be reached by a 30 minute walk along the dyke from Burghsluis.

Roompot Lock

The Roompotsluis is a new lock which provides the only passage between the North Sea and East Schelde, at the S end of Neeltje Jans island. It opens at all times and listens on VHF channel 18. The lock has sliding gates and a fixed bridge with a clearance of 18 m; and mooring pontoons with plenty of

41

Roompotsluis: entrance from seaward into Oosterschelde. Yacht mooring pontoon situated off picture to the right. Clear customs here if this is your first Netherlands landfall.

Opposite: Zierikzee town scene showing Town Hall Belfry.

sheltered sea room at each end. There is a Customs post at the lock and yachts newly arrived from seaward should report here for clearance. There is access ashore from the pontoons for this purpose.

Whether on passage to or from the Netherlands, this lock affords a convenient refuge from bad weather. If conditions preclude further progress along the coast, the inland waters can be entered instead. In good weather it is much quicker to start a homeward passage from here, rather than via the Veerse Meer and all those bridges to Flushing.

Burghsluis

Burghsluis, on the N bank of the Oosterschelde, is the first harbour on the E side of the barrier. Prior to the Delta Project it was a handy first or last port of call on a passage across the North Sea, but as chart 1805.8 shows it is now tucked away in an uninviting corner of the river. Approaching from Zierikzee, the passage is quite straightforward, and there is a conspicuous tower called the Plompetoren on the shore, less than a mile from the harbour entrance. Approaching from the Roompotsluis, the channel twists and turns round the sandbanks and a foul tide is unavoidable for part of the way. Furthermore the direction of buoyage changes during this passage and necessitates careful study of the chart.

There are pontoons on both sides of the harbour, water hoses and electricity points but no fuel pumps. The water supply is coin-operated. It is a half-hour walk to the village for shopping but the very friendly Harbourmaster will lend a bicycle. Toilets and showers (coin) are at the back of his quaint, distinctive office. A half-hour walk along the dyke will bring you to the Delta Expo ticket office and bus station, which is the best reason for visiting Burghsluis.

Zierikzee

Zierikzee is a very popular yachting centre six miles upriver from Burghsluis. Its entrance canal has no bridges or locks but beware of a strong tidal set across the entrance. About a mile up the entrance canal, pass through an open flood gate into the harbour. The pontoons at this end are all occupied by local boats. Proceed past these to the visitors' pontoon and moor alongside; if there is no space, form a trot alongside another yacht. A ramp from the pontoon leads up to the quay where a small building with a tripartite roof houses the Harbourmaster's office, toilets and coin-operated showers. Behind this is a newly restored windmill. The end of the wall behind the toilet block has a plaque showing the 1953 flood level.

Past the yacht moorings a fleet of large fishing boats moors to the quayside (Nieuwe Haven), but beyond them and the fuel barge a new pontoon has been installed where you can moor alongside if the first visitors' pontoon is full. This new pontoon has water hoses; and a toilet/shower block (coins) just by the harbour bridge.

Founded in 849 and besieged by the Spaniards in 1572, Zierikzee is a picturesque old fishing port which is said to be the best preserved town in the Netherlands. Its fine mediaeval buildings include a town hall with wooden belfry, the cathedral tower (Monstertoren) and three town gates. Across from the town hall is the oldest surviving house in Zierikzee, the Tempelierenhuis dating back to the 15th century. The narrow cobbled streets contain a good variety of shops; the quayside has chandleries, a sailmaker and most repair facilities. Market day is Thursday.

Colijnsplaat

Across the Oosterschelde from Zierikzee, the only noteworthy feature of Colijnsplaat is its excellent marina. Just 6 miles from the Roompotsluis, it is an ideal place to prepare for, or recover from, a direct passage across the North Sea.

There is a telephone on the marina reception pontoon, for visitors to notify the Harbourmaster of arrival and receive berthing instructions. Mooring pontoons have water hoses and electricity. The launderette is very well equipped (tokens) with driers and an ironing board. Full boatyard and engine repair services are available.

The town is very small and there are few shops. Although you can get all the basics, it is far better to sail across the river to Zierikzee for shopping.

Zeeland Bridge

A mile upriver from Zierikzee and Colijnsplaat, the Zeeland bridge (Zeelandbrug) is almost 3 miles long. Clearance above sea level at HW springs is 11.8 m, and up to 15 m at LW springs; gauges on the piers display the clearance at any state of tide. Yachts unable to pass under can use an opening section on the Zierikzee side of the river. Opening is at 2-hourly intervals 07–21.30 Mon–Fri; 09–21.30 Sat, Sun, hols. Exact clearance and next opening time are obtainable from the bridge keeper on VHF channel 18.

Chart 1805.5 *Zeelandbrug tot Yerseke* continues upriver from Zierikzee and Colijnsplaat. It includes: the Zandkreek passage out of the Veerse Meer; Goes; Wemeldinge at one end of the Kanaal door Zuid-Beveland which connects the East and West Schelde; and the Keeten reach of the Oosterschelde which leads NE to the Grevelingenmeer and Haringvliet.

Zandkreek

Continuing from Chapter 4, the Zandkreek lock (Zandkreeksluis on chart inset) leads from the Veerse Meer to the narrow but well buoyed Zandkreek channel. The mud banks on each side are festooned with fishing nets on stakes, and there is an abundance of water birds. At low tide the fleet of boats emerging from the lock leaves very little room, especially when others are approaching from seaward and many yachts are busy hoisting or lowering sails. Do not be tempted to get out of the way by leaving the buoyed channel as it shelves steeply.

The Zandkreek enters the Oosterschelde about 2 miles from the lock, whereupon there is a choice of three ways to go: upriver for Goes, Wemeldinge and the Kanaal door Zuid-Beveland, Yerseke, Tholen and Bergen op Zoom; under the Zeeland bridge to Zierikzee, Colijnsplaat and the Roompotsluis; or via the Keeten for Stavenisse, Bruinisse, the Grevelingenmeer and beyond.

Goes

A very high television tower at Goes is visible from afar and makes a useful landmark. From the end of the Zandkreek follow the buoyed channel S until you reach Goessche Sas, shown on the chart inset. This is immediately S of the old lock entrance, which has been dammed off since a new lock opened in 1986.

Passage to the lock is marked by port and starboard lit beacons, and the narrow entry channel (Buitenhaven) by mooring posts on the starboard side and port-hand markers on the other. There is a pontoon on the E side of the lock with access ashore for the marina facilities on the W side. The lock listens on VHF channel 18. Opening times are: Mon–Fri 6–22h; Sat, Sun, hols 8–12, 16–20h. The W (inland) side of the lock houses a new marina in the old lock approach. Its finger berths have water hoses and electricity, and extend into the old lock itself. There is a chandlery, diesel pump and showers.

From the lock, proceed 1 mile along the Havenkanaal to the village of Wilhelminadorp, where you may have a short wait before the bridge keeper arrives to wind open the swing bridge (Wilhelminabrug). Continue another mile or so in the direction of the TV tower until Goes bridge (Ringbrug) appears. This is an *ophaalbrug* and opens on the hour: Mon–Fri 07–21h (except for 12h); Sat, Sun, hols 08–11, 17–20h. You can tie up to the canal bank on either side whilst waiting.

Marinas

Immediately past the bridge on the port side is the entrance to the marina, W.V. 'De Werf'. The Harbourmaster will direct you to a berth as you enter, but in the confined space available it can be tricky to manoeuvre. This small marina is one of the most attractive in the Netherlands and has been well described as an English garden in the middle of Holland. Set in a wooded inlet, there is a neat lawn with barbecue facilities and a children's playground; while the masts, trees and nautical relics along the pathways give the whole place an atmosphere of rustic charm which is not found anywhere else. The clubhouse is draped with many familiar burgees and has a good selection of books and magazines. There are two toilet blocks with hot water, showers and a spin-drier. Hot showers and drinks from the bar are paid for by inserting the appropriate charge into honesty boxes. There is no bar service: you help yourself to drinks and do your own washing up afterwards. Readers are left to find out for themselves where the drinks are kept. At the entrance to the marina there is a miniature lighthouse which you should not fail to visit. Just like the real thing, it marks a haven to yachtsmen at a time of need.

If the marina is full, continue along the canal to the harbour bridge (St Maartensbrug). This quaint wooden *ophaalbrug* with a guardian cannon opens in concert with the Ringbrug. The harbour has box moorings on the starboard side and is surrounded by a typically Dutch scene of lovely old houses. No. 43 on the starboard side is called the 'Soepuus' and houses the unisex toilet, washing and shower facilities.

Goes town

The cobbled market place just a few minutes from the harbour has some fine 15th century buildings such as the Grote Kerk and Stadhuis, whilst pavement cafes give an atmosphere of Continental vitality. Unlike many other Dutch towns, this lively atmosphere does not disappear when the shops close; it continues late into the night. Market days are Tuesday and Saturday; most shops close on Monday but stay open late on Thursday. Beyond the market place and adjacent shopping centre is the station, where you can take day trips to Amsterdam if there is insufficient time to go by boat. A launderette at the closed end of the harbour is rather expensive. Not far from the harbour and towards the television tower is a large supermarket and a windmill. Behind the marina is an open-air swimming pool and a large park.

Every year, towards the end of July, a three-day festival is held. Boats are dressed overall and the harbour is transformed into a fairground, with market stalls, side-shows, fairy lights, live bands and dancing into the small hours.

Goes: the marina entrance showing the lighthouse where the harbourmaster waits to direct yachts to berth.

Goes: town harbour showing box moorings and 'Soepuus' to the right and alongside berths to the left.

Wemeldinge

This is the entrance to the Kanaal door Zuid-Beveland. The harbour is 3 miles upriver from Goessche Sas and looks very attractive with its two windmills. However, it has very limited moorings and is hardly worth visiting unless traversing the canal. The harbour is shown on a large scale on chart 1805.4 and has a few pontoons on its W side, N of the locks.

The Kanaal door Zuid-Beveland (chart 1805.4), otherwise known as the Hansweert–Wemeldinge Canal, cuts through South Beveland to connect the East and West Schelde. There is a lock at each end and two bridges in between. It is a handy short-cut between the two rivers and offers some good cruising itineraries. For instance, you could make a round trip by entering the Netherlands via Flushing to visit Middelburg and Veere, cruise the Veerse

Meer and go on to Zierikzee and Goes; then return through this canal to Antwerp or Breskens. Much of the commercial traffic has now switched to the new Schelde-Rijnkanaal which has fixed bridges with a clearance less than 10 m.

The locks at Wemeldinge open at all times and listen on VHF channel 18. The one to enter is indicated by an amber flashing light. About a mile up the canal there is a swing bridge (Postbrug) which opens on approach. Two miles beyond this there are two bascule bridges alongside each other, the Vlake railway bridge and a road bridge. They open hourly, but see the ANWB leaflet for exact times. There are no satisfactory waiting moorings.

Immediately S of these bridges, on the E side of the canal, a new lock should be operational in 1988. It will replace the Oostsluis which is a mile away at Hansweert, and it is hoped that it will relieve the congestion there. The Oostsluis opens at all times, (VHF channel 22). It is possible to moor to the E bank, on the canal side of the lock by the bunker boats, or to the barge mooring stage opposite. Once through the lock there is ample time to reach Antwerp or Breskens on a fair tide.

Chart 1805.9 *Yerseke tot Bergsediepsluis* is the continuation of 1805.5 and extends from the fishing port of Yerseke to the Oesterdam. The Bergsediepsluis is the lock in the Oesterdam which permits passage to the former Oosterschelde harbours of Tholen and Bergen op Zoom, and the Schelde-Rijn Canal. Since 1987, when the dam shut off the SE end of the Oosterschelde, the waters on the E side of the dam have become a tideless lake called the Zoommeer. The canal connects the port of Antwerp with the Volkerak, and is covered by chart books 1803 (see chapter 3) and 1807. However, it is effectively barred to cruising yachts as its fixed bridges are too low. The Zoommeer, Bergen op Zoom and Tholen are now included in those two chart books as they are no longer in the Oosterschelde tideway.

Yerseke

Passage upriver to Yerseke from the Zeelandbrug, past the Zandkreek, Goessche Sas and Wemeldinge, is shown on sheet 1805.5 and Yerseke harbour itself is on 1805.9. The harbour approach channel is very narrow and almost dries out at low tide, necessitating very careful attention to the buoys. The chart inset shows three separate harbour basins: the N Kon. Julianahaven is reserved for the fishing fleet; the S Prins Willem-Alexanderhaven is a marina for local yachts only; while the central Prinses Beatrixhaven has pontoons available to visitors. There are water hoses and electricity on the pontoons, toilets and showers (tokens) beneath the Harbourmaster's office. Diesel fuel is available from bunker boats in the NW corner of the Prinses Beatrixhaven.

Yerseke is renowned for its oysters and mussels, one of the reasons why the original plan to completely dam the Oosterschelde was changed in favour of a barrier which kept the river tidal. The oyster sheds and holding tanks can be seen behind the Prins Willem-Alexanderhaven. The harbour is surrounded by a very high dyke which affords some fine views but there is little that is memorable about the town. It has a small but adequate shopping centre, and a convenient take-away snack bar just a few minutes' walk from the yacht harbour.

Yerseke to the Zoommeer

Returning to the Oosterschelde fairway from Yerseke harbour, again take care to keep well within the buoyed channel. Once back in the fairway follow the buoys eastwards for 5 miles to the Tholensche Gat and the lock in the Oesterdam. This lock is called the Bergsediepsluis and has a bascule bridge over its eastern gate. It opens daily 7–21h and has a mooring pontoon on its Oosterschelde and Zoommeer sides. The lock is quite small in comparison with those described so far, and you may well find it too full to enter if you are overtaken by following boats.

Zoommeer

Charts 1803.9 and 1807.2 are identical and show the way from the Bergsediepsluis to Tholen and Bergen op Zoom, through what was once the Oosterschelde but is now the non-tidal Zoommeer. It is traversed in a N–S direction by the Schelde-Rijn Canal, while the route to Bergen op Zoom runs from W to E. This forms the marine equivalent of crossroads, with the canal as the major road. The direction of buoyage in the Schelde-Rijn canal is from S to N; but it is from W to E for Bergen op Zoom. To complicate matters further, the route to Tholen runs parallel to the northbound arm of the crossroads, alongside the Schelde-Rijn canal, and has its own set of buoys with the same direction of buoyage as the canal. It is quite easy to understand all this from the chart, but without it the collection of buoys at the intersection will make it seem more like Sphaghetti Junction. The harbours of Bergen op Zoom and Tholen are dead ends, which means that you must retrace your course to return to the Oosterschelde. This will now be against the direction of buoyage and affords scope for even more confusion. Nevertheless, Tholen and Bergen op Zoom are well worth the effort of visiting, but do make sure you have an up-to-date chart.

The Schelde-Rijn canal has enormously shortened the passage from Antwerp to the Volkerak, but is impassable to fixed-mast yachts as its bridge clearances are all less than 10 m. However, pleasure craft may use the canal and it is a far quicker way of reaching the Volkerak from this end of the Oosterschelde.

Tholen

After passing through the Bergsediepsluis into the Zoommeer, proceed along the Tholensche Gat by following the TG series of buoys. Then turn N along the Nieuwe Haven channel, following the NH buoys. This is the channel which runs parallel to, and alongside, the Schelde-Rijn Canal which is marked by beacons and SRK buoys. Take care not to stray into that very busy waterway. Because of the close proximity of these two parallel channels, some of the SRK port-hand beacons actually mark the starboard side of the NH channel, but provided the chart is carefully interpreted it is less confusing than it sounds.

The N end of the Nieuwe Haven channel bears off to port and its starboard-hand buoys must be followed carefully or you may end up in the commercial *vluchthaven* instead of the yacht harbour. The latter is well shown on the chart inset and consists of two lines of pontoon berths on each side of the entrance to the old town harbour (Oude Haven), which is not available to visiting yachts without prior permission. The pontoon berths reserved for visitors are clearly marked and there are hoses and electricity. The W.V. De Kogge clubhouse is at the N end of the Oude Haven on the town side of the dyke; it has showers and a small launderette. There is no charge for these facilities but an honesty box is provided.

The small but picturesque town has some fine old buildings and is surrounded by a defensive moat and wall, with a beautifully restored 1736 windmill on their western side. The market square is dominated by the 13th century Grote Kerk at one end and an ivy covered tower of its Catholic counterpart at the other. The 1460 town hall has a lovely belfry which plays hourly. The back of the building has a stepped gable which is best seen from the courtyard of the 1455 St Laurenskapel guesthouse. This quiet secluded area has a paved compass rose and a well-kept garden, and is reminiscent of similar courtyards in Antwerp. More stepped gables can be seen on a pair of 1622 houses in a parallel street. There is a supermarket and an adequate selection of shops scattered throughout the town.

Bergen op Zoom

Follow the TG Tholensche Gat buoys after emerging into the Zoommeer from the Bergsediepsluis and continue SE (120°) to the crossroads where the heavy traffic of the Schelde-Rijn Canal cuts across your path. This is the spot where the convergence of three different series of buoys can be somewhat confusing. Your course changes here to 065° along the Bergsche Diep channel, well marked by the BD series of buoys. Just after passing the overhead electricity lines, alter course to 035° which leads to the Burg. Pieterssluis. This lock stays open but has an *ophaalbrug* over its E end which opens Mon–Fri 6–20h; Sat, Sun, hols 7–11, 15–20h. The bridge usually opens on approach but there are mooring posts at both ends of the lock if you have to wait. The chart inset shows the short passage from the lock to the marina at the end of the Theodorushaven. It is an ugly industrial stretch and you may well wonder if it is all worthwhile; but rest assured, the 700 year old fortified city is full of interest.

Tie up alongside the visitors' stage at the W.V. De Schelde marina and report to the Harbourmaster. The toilet block next to his office has showers, and there is a diesel pump and water on the visitors' stage. Engine repairs, hauling-out and other boatyard facilities are available.

The town is 20 minutes' walk from the marina. It has an ANWB office, for charts and the railway bridge opening times. The VVV arranges guided walks through the city to see the most interesting and historic buildings: a lovely 14th century town gate, the 1537 Markiezenhof which now houses a museum, and the cobbled market square (Grote Markt) with its 1611 Stadhuis and church. The market square is surrounded by pavement cafés which give it a lively atmosphere similar to that of Goes. There is a very good shopping centre close to the market square.

Oosterschelde: Zeeland bridge to Philipsdam

Having followed the course of the Oosterschelde S from the Roompotsluis to the Zoommeer, its E arm must now be covered (charts 1805.5 and 6). This consists of reaches called, from W to E, the Keeten, Mastgat, Zijpe, Krammer and Volkerak. Prior to 1987 they were all tidal as far as the Volkerakdam, which is about 20 miles from the Zeelandbrug and has a lock leading to the Haringvliet and Willemstad. Completion of the Philipsdam in 1987 has halved this tideway and turned the Volkerak into a tideless compartment.

Chart 1805.5 *Zeelandbrug tot Yerseke* shows the start of the Keeten reach, between the islands of Duiveland to the N and Tholen to the S; and sheet 1805.6 continues as far as the Philipsdam. This dam, a final stage of the Delta Project, may well perplex yachtsmen who have not visited these parts since 1986 or bought new editions of charts 1805 and 1807. Access to the Keeten from N or S entails studying the chart to select which channel to use. The East Schelde tidal atlas should also be consulted. As in all parts of the East Schelde, care should be taken not to stray too far from the buoyed channel; and on the other hand, not to impede the passage of commercial craft which are restricted by their draft to the buoyed channel.

Stavenisse

This is not included as a place to visit, but rather as a place to avoid. Its entrance canal, on the S bank of the W end of the Keeten, is very narrow with rocky banks and dries out at LW (chart 1805.5); whilst the town itself may seem hardly worth going to. However, if the exploring instinct is predominant, the chart inset shows the way, but wait until half flood before trying to enter the canal. The flood gates beyond the entrance are kept open and half a mile onwards the canal opens out into a very large harbour basin. This is full of pontoons for local craft, most of which are small motor cruisers. There are few spaces for visitors and the lack of cruising yachts will come as no surprise after the hazards of the entrance canal. It is possible to moor to the harbour wall at its S end, but the tidal rise and fall must be allowed for. The large harbour seems to be the only favourable feature of Stavenisse. If you manage to find a vacant berth there are water hoses and electricity points. An 1801 windmill overlooks the harbour, and the town has a church tower dated 1623, a small supermarket and a few shops.

Continuing in a NE direction past Stavenisse, the Keeten then changes its name to Mastgat. At this point (chart 1805.6) there is a narrow but well buoyed branch called the Krabbenkreek which leads to the harbours of St Annaland and St Philipsland, both of which have yacht moorings but little else to recommend a visit. However, they offer a perfectly safe entrance compared with Stavenisse. Beyond the entrance to the Krabbenkreek, the Zijpe ferries will soon be seen, looking like miniature versions of the Breskens ferry. They cross the river at its narrowest point and should always be given right of way.

Just N of the ferry terminal *(Veerhaven)* on the W side of the river there is a small *vluchthaven*: this word refers to a harbour which has no marina or port facilities but affords shelter for a free overnight stay. There are many throughout the Netherlands and are intended primarily for commercial craft, but most have yacht mooring facilities. This particular one has a pontoon for yachts, and makes a useful stopping place while waiting for a fair tide. Immediately past the *vluchthaven* is the Zuid Grevelingen creek leading to Bruinisse and the Grevelingenmeer, but they belong to the next chapter.

Philipsdam

The last tidal reach of the Oosterschelde is the Krammer, which continues E from Bruinisse to the Philipsdam (chart 1805.6). This extends from the St Philipsland shore to a point halfway along the Grevelingendam, where the two join together like a T. The new dam separates the tidal Krammer from a formerly tidal reach called the Volkerak. Its Krammersluizen lock complex consists of a pair of large locks for commercial vessels and a separate one for yachts, the *jachtensluis*. The locks listen on VHF channel 22 and open at all times. The *jachtensluis* is the northernmost lock and has a mooring pontoon at each end. The Volkerak end of the lock is crossed by a fixed bridge with a clearance of 18 m. The Volkerak (chart series 1807) has a similar dam and lock complex 10 miles farther E. This leads to the Haringvliet and Hollandsch Diep and is covered in Chapter 7.

To conclude this chapter on the Oosterschelde, it must be emphasized again that in 1987 the Delta Project radically changed navigation of this river. Chart books 1805 and 1807 dated 1986 or earlier have little validity and must be replaced with current editions. In fact, since 1987, charts 1803, 1805 and 1807 have all been rearranged and retitled. Furthermore, completion of the Stormvloedkering and compartmentalization of the river by the new dams has changed the tidal patterns, so a new edition of the Oosterschelde tidal atlas is also required.

CHAPTER 6

Grevelingenmeer

Chart 1805
Until 1987 the easternmost tidal reaches originating from the Oosterschelde
were the Krammer and Volkerak, then in chart series 1807. Completion of the
Philipsdam has sealed the Krammer and made the Volkerak tideless *(fig. 12)*.
Thus it was a logical step to reallocate the Grevelingenmeer to chart 1805 as it
leads off the tidal Krammer. Series 1807 now covers only the Schelde-Rijn
Kanaal, Volkerak, Hollandsch Diep and Haringvliet. The chart revisions
commenced with the 1987 editions and include the new dams and locks, plus
extensive buoyage changes.

The Grevelingenmeer was formed in 1972 by the damming of the
Brouwershavense Gat which led from the North Sea between Schouwen and
Goeree *(fig. 5)*. The inland end is closed by the Grevelingendam between
Duiveland and Overflakkee *(fig. 6)* with the Grevelingensluis as its one and
only entry. Like the Veerse Meer it is non-tidal sea water with islands and
overnight mooring places but they are less attractive. On the other hand its
North Sea dam has better mooring facilities and access than the Veersedam.
The direction of buoyage is the same as in the Veerse Meer—from the lock to
the North Sea dam—and the 1.5 m contour is marked by withies.

Bruinisse and the Grevelingensluis
On the N side of the Krammer, at its junction with the Zijpe and just E of the
Zijpe ferry and *vluchthaven*, the buoyed Zuid Grevelingen Creek leads to
Bruinisse and, via a lock, into the Grevelingenmeer (charts 1805.6 and 7). The
E approach, i.e. from the Haringvliet and the Hollandsch Diep, is through the
lock in the Philipsdam into the Krammer.

Bruinisse is an old fishing port which was severely flooded in 1953 and has
been cut off from the North Sea by the Delta Project. Its fishing fleet now has
to operate from the Oosterschelde. The town itself has little appeal for visitors
and its main interest for yachtsmen is its lock, the Grevelingensluis, the sole
entrance to the Grevelingenmeer.

The lock opens daily 07–22h and uses VHF channel 22. Moor to the
wooden pier at the tidal end while waiting for the gates to open. There is an
ophaelbrug at the lake end. Beyond the N end of the lock there is a mooring
pontoon to starboard; and opposite, the first of two marinas at Bruinisse,
W.S.V. 'Bru', with box moorings and coin-operated showers.

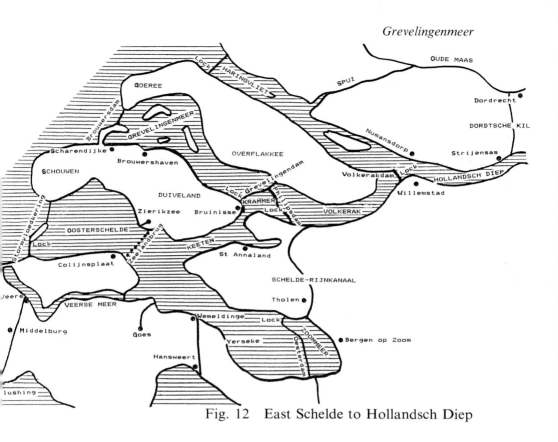

Fig. 12   East Schelde to Hollandsch Diep

From here the Grevelingenmeer is entered between two stone moles. Its ports and mooring places are described in clockwise order *(fig. 13)*. First, immediately to port, is the Aqua Delta marina on the outskirts of Bruinisse, one of the largest in the Netherlands. It has box moorings, with water hoses and electricity; and every possible facility, including a supermarket, launderette (tokens), restaurant, snack bar, shops, chandlery, and a boatyard for all types of repairs. The supermarket is very well stocked and is open until 20.30h; on Sundays it opens at 14h. Fuel is obtainable from a pontoon at the foot of the control tower. Across the road a large block of holiday flats is part of the marina development and contains an excellent shopping and recreation complex, with its own supermarket (open Sundays), swimming pool and free facilities for amusing children who are bored with sailing.

Brouwershaven

This is the most attractive port on the Grevelingenmeer. As shown on the chart inset, the entrance channel is so narrow that a one-way system controlled by traffic lights is used. The Harbourmaster's office is perched above the flood gates and he will direct you to a berth in the new marina or the old town harbour. The marina is just past the flood gates on the starboard side. It has finger berths with water and electricity, and a smart wooden

55

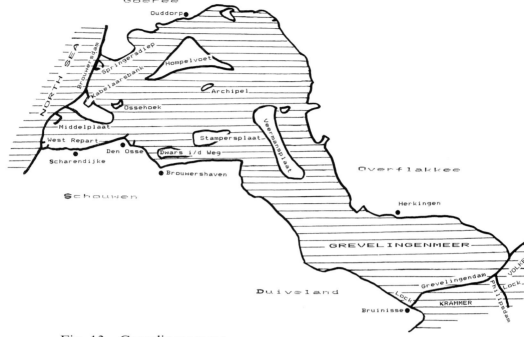

Fig. 13   Grevelingenmeer

toilet/shower block. There is a chandlery, boatyard, clubhouse and fuelling point.

Continue past the marina, along the Havenkanaal, and bear round to starboard for the old town harbour. Moor to the short stay (max. 2 hr) landing stage on the port side if you are not staying overnight. Drinking water is available there from a hose. The toilet/shower block is across the road on the starboard side of the harbour. The general scene is similar to Goes town harbour, with the yacht basin surrounded by lovely old houses. The town is small and attractive with narrow winding lanes and buildings dating back to the 14th century. Shopping is limited but quite adequate.

There is another small marina at Den Osse, at the N end of the entry channel to Brouwershaven. It has toilet and shower facilities but little else to recommend a visit.

Scharendijke

The most outstanding feature of Scharendijke is its spacious marina. The village is small and quaint. The reception stage and Harbourmaster's office face the entrance. Boats moor to box finger berths and there is a toilet/shower block. Water and fuel are obtainable from the reception stage, where it is possible to moor for a short stay. The marina has full boatyard facilities and there is a launderette in the village.

Brouwersdam

The dam between Schouwen and Goeree seals off the North Sea from the Grevelingenmeer. From its top there are fine views; and on its seaward side, superb sandy beaches which are accessible from yacht mooring places along the inland side of the dam. These allow a free stay of two days and are described from S to N as follows.

Haven West Repart is at the S end of the dam, just W of Scharendijke. The tiny harbour is noted for its floating restaurant and aquarium, but the limited number of yacht berths make it difficult to visit.

Haven Middelplaat is a larger harbour just N of the sluice gates. Despite its large area there is surprisingly little yacht mooring space.

Haven Kabbelaarsbank is similar to the previous harbour, having plenty of space but few yacht berths.

Haven Springersdiep is again similar to the previous two but has toilets and a mobile shop. It has another section on the seaward side of the dam, but there are no mooring facilities on that side.

Ouddorp

A chart inset shows this small harbour on the Goeree shore, just E of the dam. It has box moorings with water hoses but there is little space for visitors. The Harbourmaster will direct you to any vacant berths. There is a snack bar on the quayside and it is only a short walk to the village.

Herkingen

The large marina at Herkingen on the S shore of Overflakkee is shown on the chart inset. The very narrow entrance channel is marked by withies and it is important not to stray outside them or your propeller is likely to be fouled by the extensive weed beds on each side. On their arrival at the reception stage, the Harbourmaster hails visiting yachts through an intercom and allots a berth. A 2 hour shopping stay is permitted at the reception stage. The box moorings have water hoses and shower facilities. There are no fuel pumps but other boatyard services are available.

Islands

Six of the Grevelingenmeer islands have mooring facilities similar to those of the Veerse Meer. Some islands are nature reserves and one, the Hompelvoet, is closed to visitors during the nesting season, April 1–August 15.

Veermansplaat

One of the largest nature reserves, shaped like a shin bone. It has a long mooring stage on its W side, at the S end of the island, and another smaller one farther N at the westernmost point.

Stampersplaat
This nature reserve is situated halfway between Veermansplaat and Brouwershaven. The S shore of the island has a sheltered inlet with mooring stages. There is another small landing stage at the W end of the same shore.

Dwars in den Weg
Just N of Brouwershaven, with a landing stage on the S shore near the E tip of the island.

Ossehoek
The first of two artificial islands. Situated between Haven Kabbelaarsbank and Hompelvoet island, it is similar to the Veerse Meer islands. There are two tiny but well sheltered harbours, with landing stages, toilets and refuse bins. Its sandy coves and shallow pools make it an ideal spot for children.

Archipel
This is the other artificial island, situated below the concave S shore of the Hompelvoet. Although the smallest of the Grevelingenmeer islands, it is a delightful spot with three entrances to its small sheltered harbour. It also has good mooring stages, toilets and refuse bins. These two islands seem to have been made by dumping sand, and may well be a by-product of the construction work for the Brouwersdam.

CHAPTER 7

Haringvliet and Hollandsch Diep

Chart 1807

Since 1987, chart book 1807 has been entitled *Zoommeer, Volkerak en Spui, Haringvliet, Hollandsch Diep*. As shown as on the passage planning sheet 1807.1 and in *fig. 14*, the area covered in this chapter starts at the Philipsdam and extends through the Volkerak to the Volkerakdam, and thence into the Haringvliet and Hollandsch Diep.

Chart 1807.4 *Volkerak (Krammersluizen tot Volkeraksluizen)* continues E from 1805.6 of the Krammer. Craft bound E from the Krammer pass through the locks in the Philipsdam (Krammersluizen) into the Volkerak. Small craft use the *jachtensluis* and commercial vessels use the locks S of it. In addition to the traffic from the Krammer, another stream of large commercial barges emerges into the Volkerak from the Schelde-Rijn Canal, 3 miles E of the Philipsdam.

Volkerakdam

The Volkerakdam between Overflakkee and North Brabant was constructed in 1971 as part of the Delta Project. Vessels pass through the dam via a lock complex called the Volkeraksluizen, consisting of separate commercial and yacht locks.

The *jachtensluis* was specially constructed for yachts and opens at all times. It is the northernmost part of the lock complex, close to the Overflakkee shore at the end of the Hellegat. This channel is marked by the HG series of buoys, which separate it from the one leading to the commercial craft locks. Like the *jachtensluis* in the Philipsdam, there is a very long pontoon outside where you can wait for the lock to open, or stay overnight before resuming your passage.

A fixed bridge over the lock has a clearance of about 17 m, the exact figure being displayed by an illuminated sign on the bridge. Yachts requiring greater clearance may use the commercial lock (VHF channel 69) which has an opening bridge. Inside the lock, at each end, there is a 'bubble barrier', a curtain of air bubbles which rise from the bottom to prevent salt water contamination of the fresh water compartments. When in use it can have some alarming effects on your manoeuvrability if you do not have sufficient way on the boat when passing through. Beyond the lock there is another long pontoon where you can stop overnight.

Chart 1807.8 *Hollandsch Diep* continues from 1807.4 and covers the

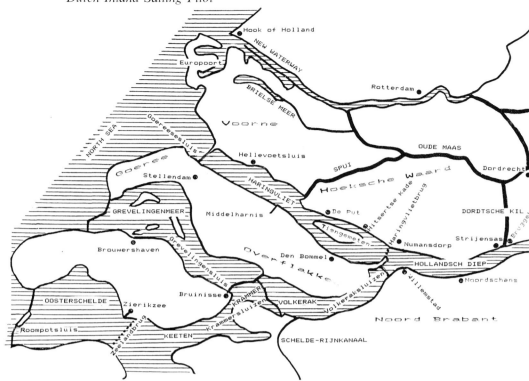

Fig. 14   Haringvliet

Haringvliet bridge, Willemstad and most of the Hollandsch Diep. From the *jachtensluis* proceed on a N course for the Haringvliet bridge and Haringvliet lake; but if bound for Willemstad or beyond, follow the eastbound channel into the Hollandsch Diep.

Willemstad

On leaving the *jachtensluis* follow the mole which protects the entrance to the commercial locks. Once past the tower at the end of the mole, Willemstad windmill will be seen to starboard on the Noord Brabant shore. As shown on the chart inset and in the Almanak, the yacht harbour is the first inlet to port as you enter Willemstad. The Harbourmaster's office is on the reception stage and he will direct you to a box berth. Drinking water is available from hoses, fuel from a barge opposite the entrance. There is a toilet block with showers. Alternatively, continue to the town harbour *(binnenhaven)*. Here it is possible to moor to the wall or alongside another boat, but it gets very crowded and it is usually more convenient to use the yacht harbour.

Volkeraksluizen: showing Hollandsch Diep side of Jachtensluis. Note the illuminated vertical clearance sign on the bridge.

The town harbour has a most attractive setting, with fine old buildings and the picturesque windmill sighted from seaward. The quayside houses are now hotels, restaurants and a chandlery; there are adequate shops. The whole town is surrounded by a high wall built in 1583 by William of Orange to keep out the Spaniards. In 1953 it kept out the sea and saved Willemstad from the fate of neighbouring communities. Built in the form of a seven-pointed star with a moat, this fortification affords a pleasant walk round the town.

Numansdorp

Willemstad is almost always crowded with yachts, and is also just as popular with landborne tourists; as a result of which the harbours are packed and the night life very noisy. Those who prefer peace and quiet should visit Numansdorp instead. Directly opposite Willemstad, on the N bank, it is a sleepy little place about half a mile up a narrow canal with no locks or bridges. Visitors moor in boxes on the starboard side. The Harbourmaster's office is on the same side, towards the end of the canal. The toilet block is in the same building, and hot showers are obtainable on payment to the office. There is a small crane for lifting masts and water-jet hull cleaning facilities. There are water hoses at the moorings and a small but good collection of shops a few minutes away.

From Willemstad or Numansdorp, the Hollandsch Diep continues E for 7 miles (chart 1807.9) before dividing into the Dordtsche Kil and Nieuwe Merwede. The Dordtsche Kil leads N to Dordrecht and is covered in the next chapter. Passage E to the Biesbosch nature reserve and Bergse Maas is restricted as the two fixed bridges at Moerdijk have a clearance of less than 10 m. Between Willemstad and the Dordtsche Kil there are three marinas which are convenient for an overnight stay before continuing to Dordrecht. These are, from W to E, at Noordschans on the S bank of the Hollandsch Diep; and at Strijensas and 'Bruggehof' on the N bank. A slender modern windmill makes an excellent landmark for the latter marina.

Noordschans is shown on sheet 1807.8, which includes an inset plan of the marina. A narrow entrance leads to a basin which is full of box moorings. Most of the usual marina and boatyard facilities are available.

Bruggehof marina is on the E bank of the Dordtsche Kil at its junction with the Hollandsch Diep. It is the smallest of the three and has box moorings and a launderette.

Strijensas

A particularly useful place if you have come all the way from Amsterdam and are determined to get through the Dordrecht bridges before catching up for lost sleep (see Chapter 9). It is the first marina to starboard after entering the Hollandsch Diep from the Dordtsche Kil, and has very good facilities, but the depth is just under 2 m.

As shown on the inset on sheet 1807.9, the entry channel is very narrow. This presents no difficulty in daylight as it is well marked with posts, but it could be tricky in the dark. Tie up at the reception stage on the starboard side and follow the signs to the Harbourmaster's office, where a box mooring will be allocated. The main facilities are all contained in one block: toilets and

Willemstad: yacht harbour looking towards town wall and windmill. Toilet/shower block situated at extreme left of picture. Entrance to harbour off right side of picture.

showers (tokens), chandlery and restaurant. There are fuel pumps, a boat lift, and a small crane for do-it-yourself mast lifting. Water hoses at the moorings.

The village is adjacent to the marina and has only a bakery, hardware store and a sailmaker. A mobile grocer visits the village and marina on Tuesday, Thursday and Saturday. A take-away chip stall is open in the marina at weekends.

Haringvliet

Chapter 2 explains the Haringvliet's crucial role in controlling water levels throughout a large part of the Netherlands. Its N end is sealed off from the North Sea by the Haringvlietdam, but there is a lock at the Stellendam end of the dam *(fig. 14)*. The direction of buoyage is from seaward towards the Hollandsch Diep, and the 2 m contour is marked by withies. Unlike the Veerse Meer and Grevelingenmeer, there are no mooring places on the islands. The River Spui leads off to the Oude Maas and the cruising grounds described in the next chapter.

Chart 1807.7 shows the inland end of the lake. Yachts coming from the Volkerak pass through the *jachtensluis* in the Volkerakdam and turn N for the Haringvliet bridge. Beyond the bridge there is a marina at Hitsertse Kade on the N shore and another opposite at Den Bommel on the Overflakkee side.

Haringvlietbrug

The bridge has a clearance of around 13 m and there are clearance gauges on the piers. Taller yachts can use the opening section at the Hoeksche Waard (N) end of the bridge, daily 09–19h. Exact clearance and opening times are obtainable from the bridge keeper by public telephones: on Tiengemeten island at the landing stage opposite Hitsertse Kade; and, from the other direction, at the Veerhaven Numansdorp half a mile E of the bridge (chart 1807.8). A very tall electricity pylon (145 m) at each end of the bridge makes it visible from a long distance.

Hitsertse Kade

This small marina is shown on the chart inset. About 2 miles from the N end of the bridge, it makes a convenient overnight stop. Boats moor in boxes which display a green board if vacant, or red if the occupier is returning. There is a drinking water hose on the reception landing stage. The single toilet block has an open unisex shower, so lock the outside door if you want to avoid embarrassment. An honesty box is provided for the shower charge. There is a small clubhouse next to the toilet block. The nearest shops are half a mile away in the village of Zuid Beijerland.

W of Hitsertse Kade, between Tiengemeten island and Hoeksche Waard, shore beacons mark a measured nautical mile and kilometre, providing a useful calibration check for your log. Continuing W, the chart inset shows a yacht berth symbol at Nieuwendijk: yachts may moor to the quayside at the end of the entry canal but there are no marina facilities. A mile beyond Nieuwendijk there is a new marina at De Put with toilets and showers.

Den Bommel

Another small marina on the opposite side of the Haringvliet, entered through a short length of canal as shown on the inset. Visitors moor to the reception stage on the starboard side. The Harbourmaster's office is at the end of the reception area, by prefabricated cabins with toilets and showers (tokens). The marina has fuel pumps, and there are shops and a bank in the nearby village.

Stad aan't Haringvliet

This village is 2 miles N of Den Bommel. The short entrance canal (chart inset) has flood gates which are kept open. Just beyond these is a tiny harbour with a few mooring boxes. The quayside is a handy place to stop for shopping or a lunch break.

Chart 1807.6 covers the harbours of Middelharnis, Hellevoetsluis and Stellendam; and the seaward entrance to the Haringvliet through the Goereesesluis at Stellendam.

Middelharnis

This is an attractive and quaint old town at the end of a mile long canal, each end of which is shown on chart 1807.6 insets. It is possible to moor in the Tramhaven at the canal entrance, but it is much better to go all the way up to the old town harbour. There is a lock and opening bridge at the canal entrance and it is necessary to report at the Harbourmaster's office by the bridge if you wish to pass through. The HM can be called on VHF channel 12, or you can moor alongside the outer harbour while seeing him. Opening times are Mon–Sat 7–22h; Sun, hols 8–22h. There is a charge for an overnight stay, but none for a day trip.

Visitors' berths are alongside the port side of the canal just before the town harbour. There are some box moorings beyond them which you may use if they are marked as vacant *(vrij)*. There is a toilet cabin by the visitors' berths;

but much better facilities, with coin-operated showers, are found in the clubhouse on the starboard side of the harbour at 15 Vingerling. There is a boatyard on the starboard side of the canal, just before the visitors' berths, where you can go alongside the fuel pumps; another boatyard on the opposite side just past the box moorings has a chandlery.

Middelharnis has a good shopping precinct and supermarket. Half-day closing Tuesday, late shopping to 21h Friday. There is a launderette at 37 West Achterweg.

Hellevoetsluis

Formerly a Haringvliet port and naval base, where William of Orange embarked for England in 1688, this small walled town is now a busy yachting centre with two large marinas. It has a few shops, a large supermarket on the outskirts and a working windmill, but lacks the charm of some other towns. It is possible to visit Rotterdam by bus.

Heliushaven yacht harbour is just W of the lighthouse which marks the entrance to the town harbour. On entry it appears to consist of one very large marina, but in fact there are three separate ones. Visitors' berths are the outermost ones and clearly marked. The box moorings have water hoses. There are toilets, showers and a launderette; plus a chandlery and clubhouse. A diesel pump is on the landing stage opposite the Harbourmaster's office. It takes about 15 minutes to walk into town.

Town Harbour is marked on the chart as the Haaven. There is a white lighthouse with a black base on the W side of the entrance. Yachts moor to the wall in trots on either side, but there are no ladders and the less agile may have some difficulty getting ashore. On the W side near the harbour entrance is a toilet block with showers. On the E side a most useful establishment, Van Leeuwen b.v. at 38 Oostkade, has a chandlery and sail loft but specializes in electronic equipment repairs.

A swing bridge across the harbour leads to another large marina in Het Grote Dok. The bridge opens daily, usually at hourly intervals, at 8–11, 11.30, 13–16, 16.30, 18, 19.30–20.30h. The marina beyond has box moorings, fuel pumps and full boatyard facilities. There is a large chandlery complete with restaurant, bar and sauna.

Koopvaardijhaven lies E of the town harbour and forms the entrance to the Voornsche Kanaal. There is a mooring stage on the W side of the harbour with toilets and showers. There are more yacht berths through the lock into the canal, but as the latter is now a dead end it seems hardly worth proceeding that far.

Stellendam

The town of Stellendam is a mile inland on the Goeree side and is inaccessible to yachts. Its importance lies in its harbour at the S end of the Haringvlietdam, which gives access to the North Sea through the Goereesesluis lock and is also the site of the Haringvliet Expo.

The inner harbour (Binnenhaven) on the inland side of the lock has no facilities for yachts. It serves the fishing fleet but yachts may moor alongside them at weekends.

The outer harbour on the seaward side of the lock has a small marina called the Aqua-Pesch Smallish Marina. The showers are coin operated, and outside the toilet block two large sinks with a coin-operated hot water supply are big enough for doing laundry or giving toddlers a bath. The pontoons have water hoses and electricity, and there is a comfortable clubhouse. There are no shopping facilities in either harbour area.

The Haringvliet Expo, an excellent exhibition of the Delta Project, should not be missed. It is housed on the dam a few minutes' walk from the lock, and yachts may be left at the pontoons on either side of the lock during a visit. Apart from the standing exhibits it includes films and a guided tour of the Haringvliet sluices, and English translations are provided throughout.

Goereesesluis

This lock has an opening bridge at each end and operates at the following times: Mon–Thurs 0–24h; Fri 0–22h; Sat, Sun, hols 8–19h. Use the pontoons while waiting. The bridge over the seaward side of the lock is high enough for most yachts, but does not have a clearance gauge. However, the clearance is broadcast by the lock keeper over a loudhailer as you approach; if in doubt use VHF channel 13.

Access to the North Sea makes the Haringvliet a useful entry or departure point on a Netherlands cruise. It is very convenient for a passage along the coast from Breskens, the Roompotsluis or Scheveningen. If weather conditions deteriorate during a sea passage, the marina in the outer harbour affords shelter. Alternatively, enter the inland waters through the lock and continue via the Haringvliet and its exits to the River Spui and Hollandsch Diep. As the lock is less than 15 miles from Hook of Holland, it makes a sound alternative to enter the Haringvliet instead and thereby avoid the dense sea traffic bound for Europoort and Rotterdam via the Hook. Rotterdam and the New Waterway may then be reached from either of the Haringvliet exits, as described in the next chapter. However, if making Stellendam your first port of entry to the Netherlands, remember that it has no Customs post, so you will have to contact the next office along your route for clearance.

The coastal passage to the Goereesesluis from N or S is covered by chart book 1801, *Noordzeekust, Oostende tot Den Helder*. The entrance from seaward (1801.4) is very well buoyed but care must be taken not to stray from the channel at LW. The chart inset shows the lock and its entrances on a large scale.

River Spui

The Spui is a tidal river which runs from the Oude Maas to the Haringvliet (charts 1807.5 and 1809.6). The direction of buoyage in the Spui is accordingly from the Maas towards the Haringvliet. This can lead to some confusion where the Spui joins the Haringvliet as they have opposite directions of buoyage. Tidal atlas *d: Stroomatlas Beneden Rivieren* gives all the required information. It enters the Voorne side of the Haringvliet, directly opposite the canal into Middelharnis (chart 1807.6).

Leaving the Haringvliet via the Spui to the Oude Maas allows a choice of going W to the Brielse Meer, Rotterdam and Hook of Holland; or E to Dordrecht and the inland route to Amsterdam. These passages are covered in chart book 1809 and the next chapter.

CHAPTER 8

Dordrecht, Rotterdam and Brielse Meer

Chart 1809
Apart from the Brielse Meer, all the waterways on chart 1809 are tidal and readers are strongly recommended to get the accompanying tidal atlas, *d: Stroomatlas Benedenrivieren*, which is based on HW Hook of Holland. Without this it is difficult to appreciate what the tide is doing at any particular point. Furthermore some bridges in the area are passable at LW but not at HW, so it is important to consider tidal patterns when passage planning.

Chart 1809.1 shows how the 1809 series continues from the previous chapter. 1809.1 shows the circular route to Dordrecht, via the Haringvliet and Spui in one direction and the Hollandsch Diep and Dordtsche Kil in the other *(fig. 15)*. Dordrecht is at the junction of three rivers: the Oude Maas, Noord and Beneden Merwede. The last leads E to the Biesbosch nature reserve and thence to Germany, but bridge clearances are only 12 m. The Noord leads to the Hollandsche IJssel, which is the inland route to Amsterdam, and to Rotterdam via the Nieuwe Maas. A round trip to Rotterdam can be made from Dordrecht via the Noord and Nieuwe Maas in one direction, and via the Oude Maas in the other. The Oude Maas also leads to the Brielse Meer, which was the first lake to be created of the Delta Project.

Identical charts 1807.9 and 1809.9 show the Hollandsch Diep joining the Dordtsche Kil. A close look at the chart will show kilometre posts along the E bank of the Kil, very useful for pinpointing your position and found on all rivers covered by series 1809. As shown on chart 1809.8 the Dordtsche Kil and Oude Maas form a Y-junction, with Dordrecht on the E arm. Here the pleasant rural scenery by the Kil changes to an unattractive industrial waterfront.

Dordrecht

The Maas is crossed by road and rail bridges on the W side of Dordrecht. The latter is a *hefbrug* and the former a double bascule bridge; most commercial traffic can pass under the road bridge but not the rail bridge, whereas most yachts require both to open. The practical consequence is that yachts are restricted on Sundays and public holidays as the road bridge only opens in the morning and evening for a limited period. On other days, both bridges open together. Another difficulty is the absence of waiting moorings. There is too much traffic to loiter in the tideway and the wash from passing barges mean that constant fending off is necessary if you tie up to the quayside. Use VHF

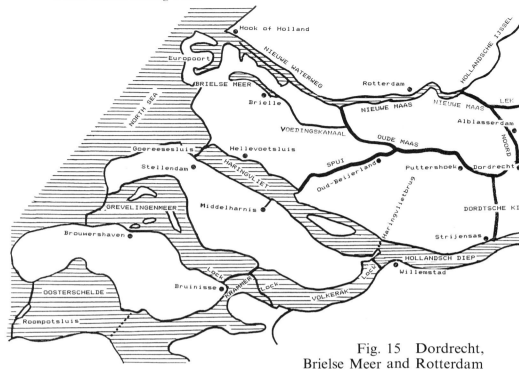

Fig. 15   Dordrecht,
Brielse Meer and Rotterdam

channel 13 if you wish to contact the bridge keeper, or Dordrecht Radio on channel 71 if there is no reply. Railway bridge opening times (see ANWB leaflet) are mainly hourly. The road bridge opens Mon–Sat 06–22h; Sun, hols 07–9.30, 18.30–21h. Once through the bridges, fuel tanks can be filled from bunker boats.

There is a choice of three entrances to the yacht harbours of Dordrecht. All have opening bridges, and suffer the same lack of suitable waiting facilities and a nasty chop from constantly passing barges. The largest and most convenient yacht harbour is the central one, in the Nieuwe Haven, which houses the Royal Dordrecht Rowing and Sailing Club. The entrance (chart 1809.8 and the Almanak) is through the Engelenburger bridge which is just E of the dominating square tower of the Grote Kerk. Opening times are Mon–Sat 09–12, 14–19h; Sun, hols 09–12, 15–20h. There is another opening bridge (Lange IJzerenbrug) across the centre of this harbour but a berth can usually be found before reaching it. This bridge gives access from the pontoon moorings to the clubhouse and Harbourmaster's office. Toilets and (coin) showers are across the road from the clubhouse. Access to boats is through a locked gate on the central bridge and a key is obtainable from the HM on payment of a deposit.

The Wolwevershaven is useful if you only need stop at Dordrecht for chandlery. The entrance is at the W side of the conspicuous Groot Hoofd town gate, and the chandlery is on the S bank between the gateway and the opening bridge into the harbour, but beware of getting your mast caught in a tree.

Until 1814 when Amsterdam was proclaimed capital of the Netherlands, Dordrecht was the most important town in the country. Its situation at the junction of Rhine and Maas waterways led to its establishment as the premier port in 1220; it has flourished ever since. Fine old merchants' homes and warehouses surround the harbour area, and three canals run through the old town which retains its historic appearance and resembles a miniature version of Amsterdam. Details of its many attractions are obtainable from the vvv by the station; the ANWB office is at 88 Spuiboulevard. Bicycles can be hired at the station. Dordrecht is a very good shopping centre. Half-day closing is Monday morning, late opening Thursday, market days Friday and Saturday. There is a launderette at 1 Spuiplein.

Charts 1809.8 and 5 show the passage from Dordrecht to Rotterdam, and the start of the inland route to Amsterdam through the Hollandsche IJssel. Proceed NE from Dordrecht past the prominent tower of an old town gate, the Groothoofd, and enter the River Noord. You may go either side of Sophiapolder island and will soon see Alblasserdam bridge. Its clearance is 11–13 m depending on the of tide, and there are gauges on the piers. Vessels requiring greater clearance may use the opening section which, like Dordrecht, is restricted on Sundays. Opening times are Mon–Sat 06–22h; Sun, hols 8.30–11, 18–20.30h. Use VHF channel 13 if necessary.

Alblasserdam

A small marina on the N side of the bridge (chart 1809.5) makes a convenient night stop on a return trip from Amsterdam or Rotterdam if you are too late to make Dordrecht or cannot get through the bridge. The entrance has an

Dordrecht: bridges across Oude Maas. Shows approach from west with road double bascule bridge and railway Hefbrug open. Fixed section to the left impassable to yachts.

Dordrecht: oude Maas waterfront as seen approaching from the north from the river Noord. Bunker boats and yacht harbour entrances are found here.

opening bridge, with a bell push to request opening at any time of the day or night. The marina has pontoon berths with water hoses but no toilet or washing facilities. The small town was destroyed during the war but has been rebuilt in an attractive style and is a busy shipbuilding centre. It has adequate shops and is within walking distance of Kinderdijk, which has 19 windmills.

Past Alblasserdam there is another marina, on the opposite side of the river, between km 983 and 984: the W.V. St Joris yacht harbour at Ridderkerk. It seems a better alternative to Alblasserdam for an overnight stay as it has all the basic facilities. The Harbourmaster provides a key for the showers and has bicycles for hire.

Proceeding N from here (chart 1809.5), the Noord ends in a T-junction with the rivers Lek to the E and Nieuwe Maas to the W with its ugly frontage of shipyards and factories. The Lek, like the Beneden Merwede, leads to the German frontier and has bridge clearances of 12 m. After turning left into the Nieuwe Maas, just beyond km 993 the Nieuwe Maas is joined on the N side by the Hollandsche IJssel, which should be entered if bound for Amsterdam. But if bound W for Rotterdam continue along the Nieuwe Maas to the Brienenoord bridge at km 995. It has a clearance of over 23 m and an opening section.

Just before the bridge, on the S bank at km 994, there is a marina at IJsselmonde. The yacht basin is surrounded by trees which screen it from adjacent shipyards. Boats moor bow to pontoon and stern to a post with a vertical rail which allows the stern warp to slide up or down with the tide. There is a boat lift should you need to be hauled out, water hoses, and a new clubhouse with toilets and showers.

Just past km 996 the river makes a U-turn and its centre is occupied by Noordereiland which carries road and rail bridges across the river. The N channel is impassable to yachts as the rail bridge clearance is only 8 m, but the S channel, called the Konings Haven, has opening sections. Like Dordrecht,

Alblasserdam Bridge: as seen from the north heading south towards Dordrecht. Opening section is at the left side of the bridge. Clearance gauges on piers at each end of fixed span.

the railway bridge is a *hefbrug* and the road bridge a *basculebrug*. Opening times are hourly 00–11h and 2-hourly thereafter until midnight, but less frequently on Sundays (see ANWB leaflet). VHF channel 13 is used.

Rotterdam

Once clear of the island, make for km 1001 on the N bank. Just past this enter the old ferry harbour *(veerhaven)* which now houses the Royal Maas Yacht Club. Tie up at the reception pontoon and report to the Harbourmaster. The moorings are set in a square inlet surrounded by trees, but this pleasant situation is made uncomfortable by wash from the unceasing barge traffic past the entrance. Showers, water hose, chandlery and a sailmaker are next to the clubhouse; and across the road is a branch of Datema, the main Dutch chart agents. It is about 20 minutes' walk from the club to the city centre. Approaching Rotterdam from the W, the yacht harbour is easy to find as it is the first inlet past the Euromast. This is just a short walk away through the park and there is a superb view from the top.

Rotterdam and Europoort constitute the world's largest port complex. Europoort is on the S side of the entrance to Hook of Holland and Rotterdam is 15 miles inland along the Nieuwe Waterweg, the only navigational hazard being the sheer density of traffic. One reason for Rotterdam's pre-eminence is its limited range of tide, less than 2 m. This allows deep-water access at all times, eliminates any need for locks, and facilitates a quick turnaround of shipping. In the last century, access to Rotterdam was indirect via Brielle or Dordrecht due to silting of the direct route; but in 1872 this was overcome by the construction of the Nieuwe Waterweg, which is a canal bypassing the original course of the river.

The city was established in the 14th century but it was not until the Ruhr coalfield was developed that it became the busiest port in Europe. Little of its

Rotterdam: entrance to Veerhaven from Nieuwe Maas; showing yacht berths at far end and (right) club house of Royal Maas Yacht Club.

architectural past remains after the bombing of 1940 which destroyed 30,000 houses. Unusually, Rotterdam has not been rebuilt in its original style of tall narrow facades with stepped gables. Instead it has been specially landscaped to give a sense of ample space while its buildings utilize the best of modern materials and technology. There are attractive office blocks and department stores, spacious traffic-free shopping precincts, museums, many fine parks and all the amenities of a busy city.

River Spui to the Oude Maas

Chart 1807.5 continues from 1807.6 and shows the exit from the Haringvliet along that end of the Spui. Chart 1809.6 shows the Oude Maas end of the Spui and the junction of these two rivers. Where the Spui joins the Oude Maas there is a choice of proceeding E and upriver to Dordrecht or W and downriver for the Brielse Meer and Rotterdam. The direction of buoyage in the Oude Maas and Spui is from seaward towards the Haringvliet and the N end of the Dordtsche Kil. Apart from the industrial areas of Rotterdam and Dordrecht, these rivers are pleasant and rural and will seem quite familiar to English east coast sailors.

The S part of the Spui (chart 1807.5 inset) has a small marina by km 1008. The Blinckvliet marina has all the usual marina facilities, though it is a half-hour walk to the village of Zuidland. Km posts 1003 and 1004 mark the entrance to the tiny harbour of Nieuw-Beijerland, but this is not recommended as it has less than a metre of water at low tide. Oud-Beijerland, opposite km 997 (chart 1809.6), is a far better place to enter for shopping or an overnight stay. Beware of the small car ferry which crosses the river at Nieuw-Beijerland by km 1003; its position is indicated by an overhead power line which is visible long before the ferry is reached.

Oud-Beijerland

The entrance is narrow, through a flood gate, and the tidal set needs care during entry. Pontoon berths available to visitors are indicated by *Vrij* signs. The pontoons have water taps but no hoses. The Harbourmaster lives on the W side of the harbour at quayside house no. 20, with a green door. The clubhouse is on the same side of the harbour, towards the entrance, at 10 Bootstraat; it has toilets, and showers with an honesty box. The town is a good shopping centre with a chandlery and sail loft, all within 5 minutes of the harbour. There are some pleasant walks through the town and on top of the dyke along the Spui.

Just past Oud-Beijerland, where the Spui joins the Oude Maas, turn E for Dordrecht, or W for the Brielse Meer and Rotterdam. En route to the latter two places there is a marina on the N bank of the Oude Maas opposite km 996, with pontoon moorings, showers and diesel.

Oude Mass westward

Continuing downriver (W), at km 1001 there is an advance clearance gauge for the Spijkenisserbrug a mile farther on. Its clearance ranges from 11 to 13 m according to the tide, but there is an opening *hefbrug* section for boats unable to pass under. It opens on the half hour Mon–Fri, but at no fixed times on Sundays and public holidays. The bridge keeper listens on VHF channel 13. There is a small marina N of the bridge at Hoogvliet, on the E bank.

Chart 1809.3 continues from 1809.6 and provides three different routes: to the Brielse Meer, to the Nieuwe Waterweg and Hook of Holland, or to the Nieuwe Maas and Rotterdam. For the Nieuwe Waterweg and Nieuwe Maas, proceed through the Spijkenisserbrug and continue N to km 1003: just past it are two more clearance gauges, one for the Spijkenisserbrug and the other for the next, the Botlekbrug. The latter is a railway bridge with a clearance of only 7 m but its *hefbrug* section opens on the hour during the same times as the former; it also uses VHF channel 13. There are no waiting facilities but there is plenty of room to keep out of the way of through traffic. These two gauges also mark the entrance to the canal which leads to the Brielse Meer. However, for the moment we are en route further N to the Botlekbrug: after passing through this it is just over a mile to the junction of the Oude Maas with the Nieuwe Waterweg to its W and Nieuwe Maas to the E.

The Nieuwe Maas eastward towards Rotterdam and beyond

Turn E at the end of the Oude Maas and enter the Nieuwe Maas. Keep away from the traffic by hugging the S bank and continue (chart 1809.4) towards Rotterdam. There is nothing but docks on either side of the river until you pass km 1003 on the S bank, onto the area of chart 1809.5. The inset portion shows the park containing the Euromast on the N bank and the first inlet E of the park is the entrance to the harbour belonging to the Royal Maas Yacht Club (page 71). One may continue E through the Koningshaven and Brienenoord bridges; thence N into the Hollandsche IJssel for the inland route to Amsterdam, or S into the River Noord towards Dordrecht.

Brielse Meer and Approaches

The previous sections have already described the passage (charts 1809.6 and 3) via the Spijkenisserbrug to km 1003 on the W bank of the Oude Maas. Just N of this post is the entrance to the canal which leads to the Brielse Meer. Turn into this entrance and moor at the pontoon while waiting for the lock (Voornsesluis). Once inside, the lock keeper will collect the charge for entry to the Brielse Meer, covering any length of stay up to 3 weeks. There is an opening bridge over the lock and mooring pontoons on the far side. About half a mile beyond the lock the Hartelbrug, clearance up to 11 m, opens in concert with the Voornsesluis: times are Mon–Thurs 8–18h: Fri 8–21h; Sat 6–21h; Sun, hols 6–22h.

There follows a pleasant and relaxing 3 mile passage along the Voedingskanaal Brielse Meer. The area to the N is a complex of oil tanks and docks, yet the canal has been so well landscaped that none of this industrial blight is visible from the cockpit of a yacht. Sheep and cattle graze on either side, and all that can be seen of the proximity of Europoort and Rotterdam are the tops of the masts of shipping passing along the parallel Hartelkanaal. Just before km 1013 there is a small marina with showers and diesel. Although called Heenvliet, it is actually a mile past that village.

Brielse Meer

The village of Zwartewaal stands at the entrance to the Brielse Meer, but its crowded little harbour has no room for visitors and no public landing places. The Meer is about 5 miles long but less than half a mile wide. Its shores have tidy grass verges and woods beyond. There are some small islands on the N side with mooring stages where one can stop overnight or picnic in quiet wooded surroundings. The Brielsemaasdam forms the N end of the lake. As this name implies, the lake was formed by damming the Brielse Maas which formerly flowed to the sea at Hook of Holland. Creation of the Brielse Meer was a preliminary stage of the Delta Project.

The only problem for yachts is a fixed bridge across the lake, one mile from the entrance. The Brielsebrug has a clearance of up to 12 m but there is no clearance gauge, and having already paid the entry fee at the Voornsesluis, it would be very annoying to find the height insufficient. The charted clearance is 10–12 m but the lake is non-tidal and levels are governed by water conservancy considerations.

Brielle

An ancient fortified port surrounded by a moat, it has a fine 15th century Gothic church and typical old houses. Enter through a narrow canal just over a mile from the Brielsebrug. It divides into two when it reaches the town: ignore the left-hand branch and go straight on to the visitors' landing stage on the port side of the harbour (Noord Spuihaven). There is a charge for an overnight stay but a shopping stop of up to 4 hours is free. If the harbour is full there is a choice of marinas at the canal entrance, half a mile from town.

The Oude Maas eastwards to Dordrecht

Charts 1809.6–8 show how to reach Dordrecht from the Haringvliet. Turn E where the Spui joins the Oude Maas. Just past km 987 on the N bank there is a marina called 'De Oude Maas' which is convenient for an overnight stop. It has pontoon berths, showers, a clubhouse and restaurant; but is half an hour's walk for shopping in the village of Heerjansdam.

Puttershoek

Just past km 984, but on the S bank, the tiny harbour of Puttershoek (chart 1809.7) is a convenient stop for shopping. The quayside is too exposed for an overnight stay, but this is possible just E of the harbour, in the Lorregat creek which has a depth of 1.5 m. Puttershoek has an excellent little shopping precinct less than 10 minutes from the harbour: there is a supermarket, bakery, butcher, chemist, and a chicken and chips take-away.

Proceeding E from Puttershoek (chart 1809.8) the pleasant rural scenery is soon lost where the Oude Maas is joined by the Dordtsche Kil. At this point one may turn into the Kil if bound for the Hollandsch Diep. Alternatively continue through the Dordrecht bridges to the town itself; or proceed into the River Noord if bound for Rotterdam or Amsterdam.

CHAPTER 9

Amsterdam

There are five routes to Amsterdam for fixed-mast yachts:

1. Inland via Nieuwe Meer
2. Inland via Haarlem
3. Inland from Den Helder
4. Via IJmuiden and the North Sea Canal
5. From the IJsselmeer

The first two routes both begin via the Hollandsche IJssel to Gouda and Alphen a.d. Rijn. The first continues direct to Amsterdam from Alphen, via the Nieuwe Meer; the second continues via Haarlem to the North Sea Canal *(fig. 16)*. The North Sea Canal is the direct sea route to Amsterdam from the coastal port of IJmuiden. It is joined by two other canals, from Haarlem in the S and Den Helder in the N; and by the River Zaan from the N. At Amsterdam the North Sea Canal joins the River IJ which gives a direct passage between the IJsselmeer and Amsterdam.

The following ANWB charts (see Chapter 1) are required. Routes 1 and 2: charts J and H. Route 3: charts F and G. Routes 4 and 5 (and the end of route 2): chart G.

ROUTE 1   Inland via Nieuwe Meer

ANWB Chart J: Grote Rivieren—Westblad
This chart includes the whole of the area of series 1809 on which the previous chapter is based. The route starts at the Hollandsche IJssel, which is close to the junction of the rivers Noord and Nieuwe Maas *(fig. 17)*. Approaching from Dordrecht via Alblasserdam and the Noord, turn W into the Nieuwe Maas. Just by km 994 on the N bank, take a sharp turn NE to enter the Hollandsche IJssel but beware of a projecting wall at the entrance. Approaching from Rotterdam, pass under the Brienenoordbrug and head NE into the Hollandsche IJssel.

The distance from here to Amsterdam is 40 miles and there are many bridges to negotiate, some of which only open at long intervals on Sundays while a few have similar restrictions on weekdays as well. Passage planning is accordingly important and is covered at the end of the route.

Amsterdam via Nieuwe Meer

Fig. 16 Fixed Mast
Routes to Amsterdam

77

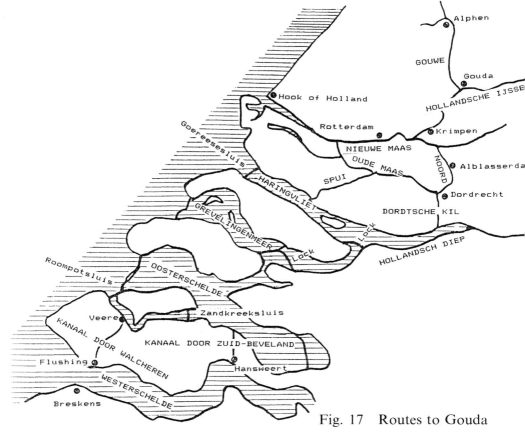

Fig. 17   Routes to Gouda

Hollandsche IJssel to Gouda

This stage is 10 miles long and the direction of buoyage is towards Gouda *(fig. 18)*.

Krimpen a.d. IJssel

This is a mile upriver from the entrance and was mentioned in the chapter on the Delta Project as the site of a key flood barrier. The barrier itself is impassable to fixed-mast yachts but there is a lock and opening bridge on its W side. The lock and its bascule bridge opens: Mon–Fri 6–6.45, 9.15–16.30, 18.30–20h; Sat 6–20h; Sun, hols 10–12.30, 16.30–19h.

Capelle a.d. IJssel

Just past Krimpen, between kms 15 and 14, the Zandrak marina on the W side of the river has pontoon berths, showers, fuel pumps and full boatyard facilities. It is not conveniently placed for shopping but does have its own small food store.

  Continuing from the Zandrak marina, beware of three ferry crossings by kms 13, 9 and 5.

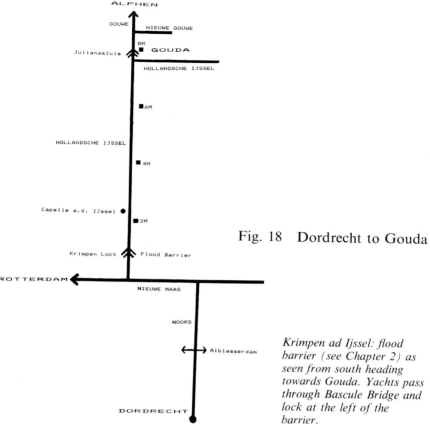

ALPHEN

GOUWE   NIEUWE GOUWE

8M
■ GOUDA

Julianasluis

HOLLANDSCHE IJSSEL

■ 6M

HOLLANDSCHE IJSSEL

■ 4M

Capelle a.d. IJssel ●

■ 2M

Krimpen Lock   Flood Barrier

ROTTERDAM ◄

NIEUWE MAAS

NOORD

◄─► Alblasserdam

DORDRECHT ●

Fig. 18   Dordrecht to Gouda

Krimpen ad Ijssel: flood barrier (see Chapter 2) as seen from south heading towards Gouda. Yachts pass through Bascule Bridge and lock at the left of the barrier.

Gouda

At km 3 the waterway divides, with the Hollandsche IJssel continuing E and the River Gouwe branching off to the N. Leave the former and enter the Gouwe. Almost immediately there is a lock with opening bridges at each end: the Julianasluis, one of the few places in this part of the Netherlands where a charge is levied. Opening times are: Mon–Fri 0–24h; Sat 0–22h; Sun, hols 6–24h. Once inside, go ashore to the office and pay the fee *(sluisgeld)*. The lock has sliding gates and listens on VHF channel 18. There are mooring posts and fuel barges at both ends.

Less than a mile beyond the Julianasluis the Nieuwe Gouwe branches off to the E. Follow this branch if you wish to visit Gouda *(fig. 19)*, otherwise continue along the Gouwe to the railway bridge.

Entry to Gouda is via the Nieuwe Gouwe and a series of opening bridges and a lock. All have the same working hours, and open on approach: Mon–Fri 6–22h; Sat 6–18h; Sun, hols closed. The first is Steve Bikobrug. Next comes a lock called Ir. De Kock van Leeuwen-sluis, tiny in comparison with anything met before, and with sliding gates. Then another bridge called the Rabatbrug (the Harbourmaster's office is situated here) leads into the Turfsingel where you can moor to the bank on either side. Alternatively, after passing through the Rabatbrug turn immediately left to the Pottersbrug and the Kattensingel where you can also moor to either bank; but beware of getting your mast caught in a tree. There are water hoses but no other facilities.

There is a small marina on the Kromme which avoids the lock and bridges. Proceed from the Gouwe into the Nieuwe Gouwe as before, but turn S into the Kromme before reaching the Steve Bikobrug. Continue down the Kromme as far as the box moorings of W.V. Gouda, which has a floating clubhouse with toilets and showers (key and tokens from the HM). Unfortunately the clubhouse is locked at night so there is no access to toilets or showers until morning. There is a water hose on the river side of the clubhouse, where you can come alongside and fill up.

The most conveniently placed of these three mooring sites is the Kattensingel as it is nearest to the shops and town centre. The shopping precinct (Kleiweg) starts at the Kleiwegbrug at the end of the Kattensingel, and leads to the market place (Markt) which is the town centre. The next most convenient is the Turfsingel; the Guldenbrug over this canal is only 5 minutes' walk from the centre. W.V. Gouda marina is about 15 minutes from the town centre.

Gouda is an ancient town which specialises in cheese and pottery. It is a lovely place and should not be missed, however anxious you may be to reach Amsterdam. The most prominent buildings, and the vvv, are found at the Markt: they include the town hall built in 1450, the Weighhouse built in 1688, and the 15th century St Janskerk which is famous for its stained glass windows and carillon concerts. Market day is Thursday and in summer the colourful cheese market is held on that morning. Horse-drawn farm carts bring the cheeses to the Weighhouse to be weighed on the original scales. Traditional costumes are worn, and there is a lively atmosphere. In the narrow side streets you may find a small pottery at the back of St Janskerk. This specialises in what may be described as fertility symbols, but they are better seen than written about. There are launderettes at 84 Karnemelksloot and 155 Graaf Florisweg.

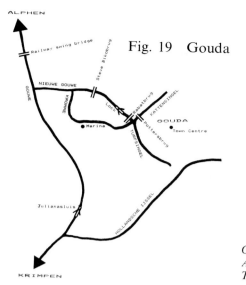

Fig. 19   Gouda

*Gouda: market place and town hall.
A cheese market is held here every
Thursday.*

Gouda to Alphen
ANWB *Chart H Hollandse Plassen*

Gouda railway bridge crosses the Gouwe just N of the Nieuwe Gouwe; it opens hourly during the following periods (but for exact details see the ANWB leaflet): Mon–Fri 6–24h; Sat 6–18h; Sun, hols 12–17h. It is 6 miles and five bridges from here to Gouwsluis, on the outskirts of Alphen *(fig. 20)*. All the road bridges listen on VHF channel 18, and open on approach: Mon 6–24h; Tues–Thurs 0–24h; Fri 0–22h; Sat 6–18h; Sun, hols 10–18h. The first is a new bascule bridge, but the others are *hefbruggen*. The railway swing bridge at Gouwsluis opens daily at all times, usually half-hourly on the whole and half-hour. Just N of Waddinxveen *hefbrug*, on the W bank, there is a supermarket and it is possible to tie up to the bank a little further on if supplies are needed. Immediately after passing the road bridge at Gouwsluis, turn W into the Oude Rijn which leads to Alphen a.d. Rijn.

Alphen a.d. Rijn

The four bridges at Alphen *(fig. 21)* open on approach, during the same hours as those over the Gouwe, and listen on VHF channel 18. The first is an *ophaalbrug* and the rest are bascule bridges. On the N side of the first, the Alphensebrug, it is possible to moor for up to 2 hours shopping at the E bank. The fourth bridge at Alphen is the 's Molenaarsbrug across Heimans Wetering. This branches N from the Oude Rijn just past the Albert Schweitzerbrug and is the direct route to Amsterdam via the Nieuwe Meer. But if bound for Amsterdam via Haarlem, you may continue along the Oude Rijn to Leiden. Alternatively, bypass Leiden by entering Heimans Wetering and leave for Haarlem at the next junction 5 miles on.

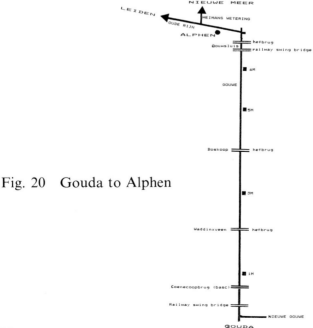

Fig. 20   Gouda to Alphen

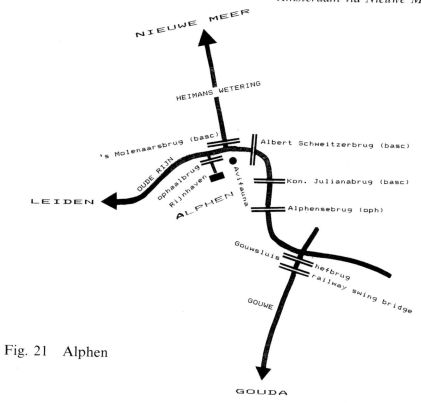

Fig. 21   Alphen

Alphen to Nieuwe Meer

It is 14 miles from Alphen to the Nieuwe Meer *(fig. 22)*. Leave Alphen through the 's Molenaarsbrug and proceed along Heimans Wetering. The bascule bridge at Woubrugge (also on VHF channel 18) is 2 miles from Alphen and opens on approach at the same times as the Alphen bridges. Just S of it there are two small marinas and a fuelling point on the W bank. Woubrugge village is a convenient shopping stop, as you can moor on the N side of the bridge, at the W bank, for 2 hours. A little further on there is a boatyard and marina on the W bank with fuel and water; and just N of these, on the E bank, is another fuelling point.

The canal then enters a small lake, the Braassemermeer, in which the direction of buoyage is from S to N. Just S of the entrance to this lake, watch out for a pedestrian ferry. There are marinas at each end of the lake, with fuel pumps and all facilities. At the N end, where the lake joins the Oude Wetering, beware of a small car ferry. It is possible to moor on the W bank of the Oude Wetering for shopping; there are also chandleries and a sailmaker. About a mile on, the Oude Wetering ends at a T-junction with the Ringvaart van de Haarlemmermeerpolder, the eastbound arm of which is the direct route to Amsterdam via the Nieuwe Meer. The westbound arm through the Weteringbrug is the indirect route via Haarlem: going this way, rather than from Alphen via the Oude Rijn, saves time as it bypasses Leiden *(fig. 24)*.

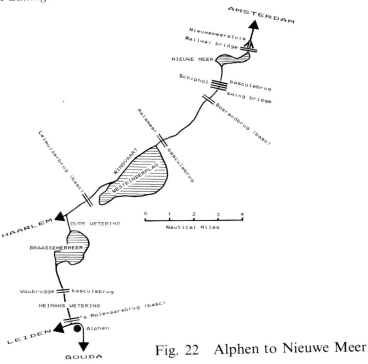

Fig. 22   Alphen to Nieuwe Meer

Ringvaart van de Haarlemmermeerpolder

As the name implies, *ringvaart* means a circular canal. Here the 25 mile circle encloses a former lake, the Haarlemmermeer *(fig. 32)*, which once extended to the E side of Haarlem. The lake was a potential flood threat to Amsterdam, Leiden and Haarlem and accordingly plans were made as far back as 1640 to drain it. But it was not until the advent of steam power that this was finally achieved in 1852. The reclaimed *polder*, the Haarlemmermeerpolder *(fig. 16)*, is 4 m below sea level and traversed by a geometrical pattern of roads and drainage canals. It is now occupied by farms and Schiphol Airport, to be seen below your level, on the former bottom of the lake, as you proceed along the *ringvaart*.

Turn right from the Oude Wetering into the eastbound arm of the *ringvaart*. There is another fuelling point on the S bank by km 12. A mile on, *(fig. 22)* Leimuiderbrug opens on approach: Mon 5–24h; Tues–Thurs 0–24h; Fri 0–22h; Sat 6–20h; Sun, hols 8–13, 14–20h. Yachts can moor to the N bank on either side of this bridge.

The *ringvaart* continues round the edge of a 3 mile long lake, the Westeinderplas: it can be entered from the *ringvaart* and contains several marinas and quiet places for an overnight stay. On the W bank near km 50 there is a small supermarket with a landing stage; and a little farther on, by the Rijsenhout pedestrian ferry, is another mooring place where a 2 hour stop is allowed. There are a small supermarket, baker, butcher, greengrocer, and bank just a few minutes away. At the end of the lake the *ringvaart* passes between Aalsmeer, on the S bank, and Schiphol Airport. The bascule bridge at

Aalsmeer opens on approach, at the same hours as that at Leimuiden. There is a diesel pump on the S bank at the E side of the bridge.

Aalsmeer

This is the flower-growing centre of the Netherlands. It produces cut flowers, whereas the bulbfields, between Haarlem and Leiden, concentrate on the cultivation and sale of bulbs. The S bank of the *ringvaart*, from Westeinderplas to just beyond Aalsmeer, is penetrated by narrow waterways which irrigate and enrich the soil for the flowers. Unfortunately, little can be seen of them as most are grown under glass. However, you can stop at Aalsmeer and visit its morning flower auctions, the town's most popular attraction.

Just over 2 miles from Aalsmeer, the Bosrandbrug opens during the same hours as the previous two bridges, except for: Sat 6–22h; Sun, hols 8–13, 14–22h. Half a mile further on are the last two bridges before the Nieuwe Meer: the Schiphol road bridges. They only open for short periods, with long intervals between: Mon–Fri 5–6.30, 12.30–13.30, 20–21h; Sat 7–8, 12.30–13.30, 19–20h; Sun, hols 8–10.30, 18.30–21h. There are limited moooring facilities on each side of the bridges. Beyond them, it is just a mile to the Nieuwe Meer.

Nieuwe Meer

The Nieuwe Meer is a small lake just over a mile long which branches off from the *ringvaart*. The direction of buoyage is from Amsterdam to Schiphol. Set in pleasant wooded surroundings, it is the home of large numbers of great crested grebes. At the far end of the lake the Nieuwemeersluis leads to the Amsterdam waterfront via a 4 mile stretch of canal with 11 bridges. The first and tenth are railway bridges which only open once a day, around midnight. As the Nieuwe Meer is only a short bus ride from the city centre, there is little point in proceeding any further unless you intend cruising the IJsselmeer or returning via the North Sea Canal. If Amsterdam is your only destination and you intend returning the same way, it is far simpler and more comfortable to stay at a marina in the Nieuwe Meer and visit Amsterdam by bus.

There is a choice of marinas in the lake but the most convenient and friendliest is the W.V. 'de Koenen', at the E end just S of the railway bridge. It has a small chandlery, a clubhouse with showers, and box moorings with water hoses. The harbourmaster lives on a houseboat and does not charge for the first night's stay. It is ten minutes' walk from the marina to the bus stop; a 170 or 172 bus goes to Amsterdam's Central Station. On the return ride, if you cannot remember where to get off, ask the driver to announce the Jollenpad, which is just past the Olympic stadium and the bridge over the Nieuwemeersluis.

Nieuwe Meer to Amsterdam

A canal called the Schinkel leads from the Nieuwe Meer to the Houthaven on the Amsterdam waterfront *(fig. 23)*. The railway bridges at each end of the passage open for a single period around midnight each day, so a special one-way system is used:

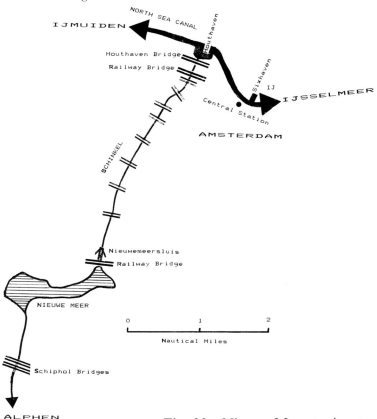

Fig. 23   Nieuwe Meer to Amsterdam

(a)   Be ready to leave the Nieuwe Meer by 23h. (There is a mooring stage by the bridge.) For information on the exact opening time, call the lock keeper on VHF channel 22.
(b)   Just after 23h the railway bridge over the Nieuwemeersluis opens.
(c)   Move through the sliding gates into the lock. The mooring points inside are convenient, and a water hose is available. A fee for the passage into Amsterdam must be paid at the lock office.
(d)   When all the boats are inside, the lock is operated and the whole fleet of boats proceeds along the canal.
(e)   Each bridge opens in turn as the fleet approaches.
(f)   The penultimate bridge is the second railway bridge, just before the Houthaven. Once the fleet has passed through, the waiting southbound convoy starts its passage to the Nieuwe Meer.

In practice the journey through this series of bridges is by no means easy. It all takes place at night and the convoy is usually large. There is a constant risk of collision as the fastest boats arrive before the next bridge opens and have inadequate space to manoeuvre without getting in the way of the following ones. Furthermore the water contains a profusion of plastic bags and other floating rubbish which presents the additional risk of a fouled propeller.

Having arrived at the Houthaven in the small hours of the morning, you may wish to snatch a few hours' sleep there before resuming your passage at daybreak. If so, there is a mooring stage in the SW corner, on the N side of the Houthaven road bridge. If you wish to stay in Amsterdam, the best place is the Sixhaven yacht harbour opposite the Central Station (described at the end of this chapter, in the section on Amsterdam city).

Amsterdam to Nieuwe Meer

For a passage from Amsterdam to the Nieuwe Meer, the railway bridge openings will be some time after midnight. The passage starts on the Amsterdam waterfront at the entrance to the Houthaven. This is best shown on ANWB chart G, *Amsterdam—Alkmaar,* which is the one used for routes to Amsterdam from the IJsselmeer, IJmuiden and the North Sea Canal. The Houthaven is on the S bank, just over a mile E of km 20. From the IJsselmeer direction, it is a mile W of the Sixhaven yacht harbour and the Central Station.

Enter the Houthaven and proceed to the road bridge at the SW corner. Tie up at the mooring stage and go ashore to the bridge office, where you must pay the passage charge and find out exactly what time the railway bridge is due to open. There is a water hose at the mooring stage. The road bridge opens periodically to let the inward bound convoy assemble and wait at the first railway bridge. There are no special mooring facilities and you have to lie against the canal wall. If you arrive early, be sure to set an alarm clock: if you fall asleep and miss the opening there will be a 24 hour wait for the next one! When the bridge opens the convoy proceeds through, and all subsequent bridges to the Nieuwe Meer lock open on approach. Once all the boats are secured inside the Nieuwemeersluis, the last railway bridge opens and the Nieuwe Meer lies beyond.

Passage Planning

The most important things to remember about the inland route to Amsterdam via the Nieuwe Meer are that most bridges have restricted opening on Sundays and public holidays, while Schiphol bridge only opens three times a day on weekdays and twice on Sundays. Although the route begins at the Hollandsche IJssel, you may well be starting from somewhere else. If coming from the S, the bridges over the Oude Maas at Dordrecht have very restricted opening times on Sundays and holidays; so too does the bridge over the Noord at Alblasserdam if your clearance is more than 12 m. These Sunday opening times are in the morning and evening only, for just a few hours. Furthermore the rivers are tidal as far as the Hollandsche IJssel and this must be borne in mind when estimating passage times.

The journey from Krimpen lock to Schiphol takes about 9 hours at 4–5 knots, and you must be at Schiphol in time for one of its few openings. If your ETA at Schiphol means a wait of several hours, it would be better to pass that time by stopping somewhere else between Alphen and Aalsmeer where there are better mooring facilities and somewhere nice to go ashore.

Similar considerations apply when going S from Amsterdam via the Nieuwe Meer. Starting an hour or two after midnight, you will probably arrive at the Schiphol bridges at about 05h whereupon some more waiting is necessary before they open. To get beyond Dordrecht in one day you must get through the Dordrecht bridges over the Oude Maas. This entails a long passage of 40 miles and by the time you are through these bridges it will probably be about 18h, and you may well want to catch up on some sleep at the first available marina. The nearest ones are at Heerjansdam on the Oude Maas, and Bruggehof or Strijensas on the Hollandsch Diep.

ROUTE 2   Inland via Haarlem

ANWB Chart H: Hollandse Plassen

There are two different ways of starting this route. The first is from Alphen a.d. Rijn, via the Oude Rijn, to Leiden and thence to Sassenheim. The second, and quicker, way goes from Alphen direct to Sassenheim, via Weteringbrug and the westbound arm of the Ringvaart van de Haarlemmermeerpolder *(fig. 24)*. At Sassenheim both ways unite and proceed straight to Haarlem. The passage as far as Alphen or Weteringbrug has already been described under Route 1.

Alphen to Leiden

It is 7 miles from Alphen to Leiden. After passing through the Albert Schweitzerbrug at Alphen, continue W along the Oude Rijn past the Avifauna International Bird Park on the S bank *(fig. 21)*. It is well worth visiting: some 10,000 birds live in gardens which recreate their natural environment. It is possible to moor alongside the river bank by the entrance to the Avifauna, where the tourist boats arrive, but it is exposed to the wash of passing traffic. A better overnight stop is in the Rijnhaven industrial harbour on the W side of the Avifauna; it is entered through an *ophaalbrug* which opens: Mon–Fri 6.45–7.30, 9–16.30, 18–19h; Sat 6.45–7.30, 11.30–13h; Sun, hols closed. As the Rijnhaven is for commercial craft there are no special facilities for yachts, but you can moor alongside the wall at the far end. Apart from the Avifauna, there is little to stop for at Alphen, and it has no marina. A shopping stop can be made by the Alphensbrug.

The next bridge is just over 2 miles from Alphen at Koudekerk a.d. Rijn *(fig. 24)* but just before reaching it there are two mooring places on the N bank of the river. The first is opposite a road called Pr. Wilhelminastraat which leads to a small shopping centre with a supermarket, bakery, post office and banks. The second is almost next door to a 'chips with everything' takeaway. Opening times of the *ophaalbrug* at Koudekerk are: Mon–Fri 6–22h; Sat 8–18h; Sun, hols 10–18h. There is another mooring place on the W side of the bridge, by a garage on the S bank; and 2 miles on, some more mooring places on the N bank. Just over half a mile from these is the town of Leiderdorp, on the outskirts of Leiden.

The first bascule bridge at Leiderdorp opens: Mon–Fri 6–8, 10–16.30, 18.30–20h; Sat 9–14h; Sun, hols closed. The second (Leiderdorpsebrug) opens: Mon–Fri 6–7, 9–16, 18–21.30h; Sat 9–18h; Sun, hols 11–15h. Just N of the Leiderdorpsebrug a branch of the Oude Rijn called the Nieuwe Rijn flows W through Leiden. A little further on the Oude Rijn gives off a northbound branch called the Zijl and then turns W through Leiden to join up again with the Nieuwe Rijn at the town centre.

Leiden itself has no yacht mooring facilities, but the town is well worth visiting. At the junction of the Zijl and Oude Rijn, enter the Zijl through the

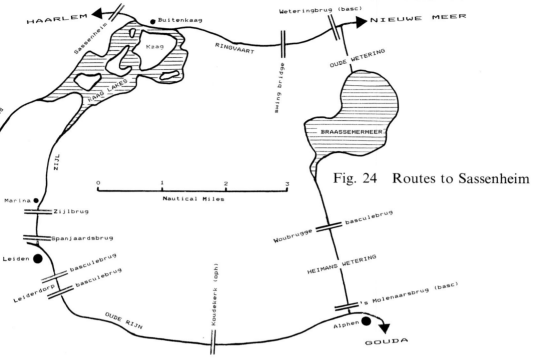

Fig. 24   Routes to Sassenheim

Spanjaardsbrug, open: Mon–Fri 6–7, 9–16, 18–21.30h; Sat 9–18h; Sun, hols 11–15h. The next bridge, half a mile away, is the Zijlbrug which opens: Mon–Fri, same hours as Spanjaardsbrug; Sat 9–14h; Sun, hols closed. There are mooring posts on its S side.

Once through this bridge, the 'Zijlzicht' marina straight ahead is the most convenient stopping place for a visit to Leiden. It has box moorings, water hoses, fuel pumps, a chandlery and boatyard. A small toilet block with (coin) shower is behind the workshops and chandlery. A mobile grocery visits the marina at weekends. It is a good half-hour walk to Leiden town centre but there is a bus service to the railway station from quite near the marina.

Leiden

In 1574, Leiden sprang to fame when it withstood a long siege by the Spanish. In appreciation of the loyalty and courage of its citizens, William of Orange endowed the city with a university which soon became a world-famous centre of learning, especially in the fields of medicine and law. Rembrandt was born in Leiden in 1606; and in 1609 the Pilgrim Fathers were given refuge there. By 1670 it was the second largest city in the country and a centre of the textile industry. Many buildings and monuments dating back to those times can still be seen. The vvv opposite the station issues a booklet which gives a walking route through the old town and university quarter and describes the historic buildings. Leiden is also an excellent shopping centre and has an ANWB office and sailmaker. Market days are Wednesday and Saturday. Bicycles can be hired from the railway station.

Leiden to Sassenheim

This section of the route is 4 miles long. From the Zijlbrug or Zijlzicht marina proceed N along the River Zijl for 2 miles until it enters the Kaag lakes. These are called Kager Plassen on ANWB chart H and shown on a larger scale on the inset section. It is well worth staying for a while in this delightful area. Yachts drawing 2 m can pass through the lakes via a channel marked by light beacons. Outside this channel, the chart inset shows several shallow patches.

The expanse of water contains five islands which make it seem like several adjoining lakes. The islands and lakesides are polders and dotted with picturesque windmills and grazing cattle. This rustic setting seems to have far more charm than the Veerse Meer and other lakes created by the Delta Project; however the Kaag lakes share with the Veerse Meer the distinction of being among the most popular yachting centres in the Netherlands. At weekends throughout the summer they are teeming with yachts: there are several clubs and a great deal of racing takes place. These sheltered waters are also very popular for weekend cruising and large numbers of boats anchor overnight as the lakes do not have the island mooring places or variety of marinas which characterize the Veerse Meer. Most boats buoy their anchors.

Two useful spots to visit are Warmond at the SW corner and Kaag Island at the NE. Warmond has landing stages on each bank, by the fixed bridge, where you are allowed to stay for 3 hours: ample time for a meal break and shopping in the village. There are several marinas and boatyards where all repairs can be undertaken. Kaag Island has a large marina on its N side opposite Buitenkaag, the Jachthaven Kaagdorp. It has box moorings with water hoses, a toilet block and (coin) showers. There are some other small marinas and mooring places, but most cruisers seem to anchor overnight.

The N end of the lakes, at the village of Buitenkaag, is traversed by the Ringvaart van de Haarlemmermeerpolder, and this forms the meeting point of the direct and indirect routes to Haarlem. Here the direct route to Haarlem, from Alphen to Weteringbrug and then W along the *ringvaart*, joins the indirect route via Leiden and the Kaag lakes. From this N end of the lakes proceed NW along the *ringvaart* for under half a mile to the Sassenheim bridges. An account of the route from there to Haarlem will be given below, after a description of the direct passage from Alphen to Sassenheim.

Alphen to Sassenheim

This direct route is 9 miles long, but it really starts at Weteringbrug where the Oude Wetering joins the *ringvaart (fig. 24)*. The passage from Alphen to Weteringbrug has already been covered in Route 1 via the Nieuwe Meer. At Weteringbrug the latter route takes the eastbound arm of the *ringvaart*, while the route via Sassenheim and Haarlem takes the westbound arm. Immediately after entering the westbound arm, pass through the Weteringbrug, which opens: Mon–Fri 6–22h; Sat 7–21h; Sun, hols 9–13, 14–20h. There are mooring stages at the N bank on each side of the bridge.

Proceeding W from the Weteringbrug, past a windmill on the S bank the *ringvaart* crosses a road by means of an aqueduct before reaching the Meerbrug at Nieuwe Wetering. This is about a mile from the Weteringbrug and opens during the same hours, except for Sun and hols: 8–13, 14–21h. It is a hand-operated swing bridge and the keeper lowers a clog on a fishing rod as you pass through, so have some coins ready. Continue W past the houseboats on the S bank to the hamlet of Huigsloot, where you can moor to the N bank for 3 hours, though there seems little to stay for apart from a restaurant and garage. After another mile the *ringvaart* joins the route from Leiden at Buitenkaag on the N end of the Kaag lakes. Buitenkaag has a few shops, a chandlery, fuel pumps and a small car ferry to Kaag Island; it is possible to moor to the N bank of the *ringvaart*. From here it is less than $\frac{1}{2}$ mile W along the *ringvaart* to the Sassenheim bridges.

(left) Kaag Lakes: typical scene on one of the islands in this attractive area of the Netherlands.

(above) Warmond: the author's catamaran is moored at the short stay landing stage where a three hour stop is allowed.

Sassenheim to Haarlem

There are two adjacent bascule bridges across the Ringvaart van de Haarlemmermeerpolder at Sassenheim. They open together, for three brief periods on weekdays but only once on Sunday. Exact times are in the ANWB leaflet but approximate to: Mon–Fri 6–7.15, 12.30–13.15, 18.45–19.30h; Sat 10.15–11, 14.15–14.30, 19h; Sun, hols 17.15–17.30h. There are mooring places on the E bank on both sides of the bridges, but as they open so infrequently a wait of a few hours can more enjoyably be spent sailing the Kaag lakes. There is a marina and boatyard with fuel pumps on the N side of the bridges at the N bank. It is 11 miles from here to Haarlem.

The next bridge is 2 miles away at Lisse *(fig. 25)*, the centre of the bulbfields and opens: Mon–Fri 7–21h; Sat 9–17h; Sun, hols 10–12, 16.30–18.30h. There is a marina on the S side of the bridge at the W bank. On the N side at the E bank, by km 5, a small supermarket has its own landing stage. The Hillegommerbrug, just over 2 miles from Lisse, opens during the same periods as the Lisserbrug, except for Sun and hols: 9.30–11.30, 17–19h. Continuing N along the *ringvaart* for another 2 miles, the next bridge is the Bennebroekerbrug, open at the same times as the previous two except for Sun and hols: 9–11, 17.30–19.30h. The last bridge before leaving the *ringvaart* is 2 miles on at Cruquius; this *ophaalbrug* opens: Mon–Fri 7–22h; Sat 8–17h; Sun, hols 8.30–10.30, 18–20.30h.

Cruquius is the site of one of three pumping stations which drained the Haarlemmermeer. It was in continuous use for 84 years, from 1849 to 1933, and is now a fascinating museum which contains the original English steam pump which did most of the work. Working models show how windmills and steam pumps drained the polders; also a relief map of the Netherlands is alternately flooded and drained to show the original coastline and reclaimed areas. The museum is at the E side of the bridge on the S bank of the *ringvaart*. There is a pleasant tea house next door with a landing place for waterborne museum visitors.

Immediately past the museum the waterway divides into two: the Ringvaart van de Haarlemmermeerpolder continuing NE, and the River Spaarne running N. The latter waterway is the route through Haarlem, the rest of the *ringvaart* being impassable to fixed-mast yachts.

Haarlem

The Cruquius end of the River Spaarne is called the Zuider Buiten Spaarne and soon leads to the first of eight bridges through Haarlem *(fig. 26)*, numbered 1 to 8 from N to S on the ANWB chart. Opening hours for all of them are: Mon–Fri 9–16, 18–21h; Sat 9–18.30h; Sun, hols 17–19h. Once through the first, all the rest open on approach.

The first bridge is a mile from Cruquius, at Heemstede on the outskirts of Haarlem: no. 8, the Schouwbroekerbrug. If it is closed and unmanned, or displaying two red vertical lights, call Haarlem Harbour Control on VHF channel 18 and they will tell you when the eight-bridge system will be open. If you wish to stop overnight before passing through these bridges, there is a small yacht basin immediately SW of the Schouwbroekerbrug at the mouth of

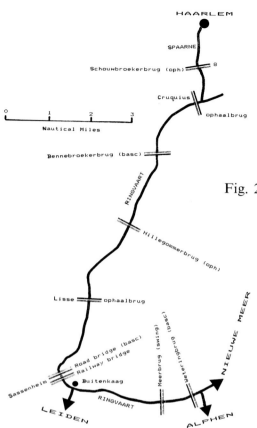

HAARLEM

SPAARNE

Schouwbroekerbrug (oph)   8

Cruquius

ophaalbrug

0   1   2   3
Nautical Miles

Bennebroekerbrug (basc)

Fig. 25   Sassenheim to Haarlem

RINGVAART

Hillegommerbrug (oph)

Lisse   ophaalbrug

NIEUWE MEER

Road bridge (basc)
Railway bridge

Meerbrug (swing)

Waterringbrug (basc)

Sassenheim   Buitenkaag

RINGVAART

LEIDEN

ALPHEN

*Cruquius: approaching bridge
from Haarlem building, at left
is the former pumping
station—now a museum.*

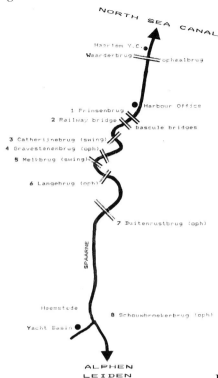

NORTH SEA CANAL

Haarlem Y.C.
Waarderbrug
ophaalbrug

Harbour Office
1 Frinsenbrug
2 Railway bridge
bascule bridges
3 Catherijnebrug (swing)
4 Gravestenenbrug (oph)
5 Meltbrug (swing)

6 Langebrug (oph)

7 Buitenrustbrug (oph)

SPAARNE

Heemstede
8 Schouwbroekerbrug (oph)
Yacht Basin

ALPHEN
LEIDEN

Fig. 26   Haarlem

the Haven Kanaal. It has no facilities but is only 10 minutes from the shops, through a modern housing estate whose streets are all named after composers. The basin has a block of flats on one side, but the opposite bank of the canal has a pleasant rural aspect of open fields, grazing cows and numerous oystercatchers, herons, coot and ducks. Cruquius museum is a short walk from here, or you can get a no. 140 bus from the main road a few minutes away and get off at Cruquius bridge.

Continuing N from the Schouwbroekerbrug past some splendid riverside dwellings on the W bank, bridge no. 7, the Buitenrustbrug, is a mile on and has a mooring stage on its SW side. The remaining six bridges are in the next mile of river as it flows past the city centre. It is possible to moor on the E bank between bridges 5 and 6. No. 4, a fine old *ophaalbrug* called the Gravestenenbrug, is one of Haarlem's tourist attractions. There is a mooring place at the bank on the S side of no. 3, the Catherijnebrug, and a fuel barge between bridges 2 and 3 on the N bank. The last of the series, the Prinsenbrug, is close by the railway bridge and opens in concert with it (see ANWB leaflet). Moor to the quay or alongside another boat while waiting. After passing through the Prinsenbrug, tie up alongside the harbour office on the W bank to pay the Haarlem harbour dues. The same applies to boats coming from the opposite direction.

The remainder of the inland route to Amsterdam via Haarlem is covered by ANWB chart G *Amsterdam—Alkmaar*.

94

Continue N for half a mile, away from the city centre, to the Waarderbrug, which opens during the same hours as the rest of the Haarlem system. There is a landing stage at the W bank on the N side of the bridge. Haarlem Yacht Club marina is $\frac{1}{2}$ mile N of this bridge on the W bank, and visitors are made very welcome. It has fuel pumps and a water hose at the entrance, with box moorings and a small boatyard inside. Showers are available beside the clubhouse (pay at the bar). This is the best place to stay if you wish to visit Haarlem. There is a small shopping centre about 10 minutes from the marina: turn right outside and then left at the traffic lights. Alternatively there is a large supermarket about 20 minutes in the opposite direction: turn left outside the marina and walk along the riverside to just past the Waarderbrug, where you will see the supermarket across the road. Continue another 20 minutes along this main road (Spaarndamseweg) to reach the town centre. If you prefer to ride, catch a no. 4 or 5 bus from the stop opposite the marina entrance: this goes to the bus station, which is in the same square as the railway station, vvv and ANWB offices. The vvv issues a very good town plan with details of the most interesting places to visit.

Haarlem became established as a flourishing city in the early Middle Ages and has some fine mediaeval buildings in the market square. The most outstanding are the town hall, the meat hall (Vleeshal) and St Bavo's church (Grote Kerk). Building of the church commenced in 1390 and took a hundred years. It contains the tombstone of Franz Hals; and is also famous for its organ, which dates back to 1738 and was played by Mozart and Handel. Market days are Monday and Saturday. Like most Dutch towns it has an excellent pedestrianised shopping centre; and on the N side of the market square in the Brinkman Passage, a magnificent indoor shopping precinct complete with genuine red GPO telephone booths. The Cruquius museum can be visited by taking a no. 140 bus from the station.

Haarlem: heading south through the city towards Cruquius; showing Belfry of St Bauo's Church (Grote Kerk).

Haarlem to Amsterdam
ANWB Chart G: Amsterdam—Alkmaar

This part of the route is in two sections: the 4 miles from Haarlem to the North Sea Canal, and another 8 from there to Amsterdam *(fig. 27)*. From Haarlem Yacht Club the river flows NE for a mile to Spaarndam. This part of the river is called the Noorder Buiten Spaarne, and a small lake called the Mooie Nel on its S side has two marinas with all facilities, but depths are less than 2 m. It makes a sheltered overnight stopping place if you are not visiting Haarlem or are too late for the next bridges. At Spaarndam, just past the entrance to the Mooie Nel, a lock with an *ophaalbrug* at its N end listens on VHF channel 18, and opens: Mon–Fri 6–22h; Sat 6–20h; Sun, hols 7.30–10, 17–21h. The lock has low walls, which makes it easy to get ashore and pay the lock keeper in his office on the bridge. There is a small marina at the S end of the lock on the W bank.

Beyond the lock, the waterway is tidal and is called Zijkanaal C. Its direction of buoyage is from the North Sea Canal to Spaarndam. Half a mile from the lock it is crossed by a bascule bridge which only opens during three periods a day: Mon–Fri 5.45–7, 12–13, 20–21h; Sat 7–8, 12–13, 16.45–17.15h; Sun, hols 8–9, 17.30–17.40, 20.40–20.50h. Just before it enters the Noordzee Kanaal, Zijkanaal C is crossed by an *ophaalbrug* at Buitenhuizen. Opening times are: Mon–Fri 5–23h; Sat 5–21h; Sun, hols 7–7.50, 9.10–10.30, 17, 18, 20.10, 21h.

From here turn E into the Noordzee Kanaal and continue in that direction all the way to Amsterdam, with no more bridges or locks to negotiate. There is heavy traffic throughout the Noordzee Kanaal so look out for the superstructure of approaching shipping as you leave Zijkanaal C. Beware, too, of the Buitenhuizen car ferry which crosses the Noordzee Kanaal at this point (km 10). The passage along the Noordzee Kanaal to Amsterdam will be covered in Route 4, IJmuiden to Amsterdam.

On the S side of this last bridge is the W.V. IJmond marina, on the W bank of Zijkanaal C. The harbourmaster is most helpful and speaks very good English. There are showers and a launderette (tokens from the HM). The clubhouse has a restaurant with far cheaper meals than one generally expects, and provides take-away dishes too. This is the first marina along the Noordzee Kanaal and an excellent stopover after a direct sea passage to IJmuiden, allowing a rest before proceeding to Amsterdam. Engine repairs can be undertaken by a local marine engineer. It is 10 minutes' walk from the marina to the Buitenhuizen ferry, where there is a half-hourly bus service (no. 82) for the half-hour journey to Amsterdam. In the opposite direction, the bus takes 10 minutes to IJmuiden, which is the nearest place for shopping (get off at Plein 45).

Passage Planning
Planning a passage to Amsterdam via the Nieuwe Meer has already been described. The route via Haarlem entails the same considerations of bridge opening times, especially on Sundays. Most road bridges between Alphen and Leiden are closed on Sundays and public holidays; but that stretch can be avoided by taking the direct route from Alphen to Sassenheim. Whether going via Leiden or not, the Sassenheim bridges must be passed and they only open

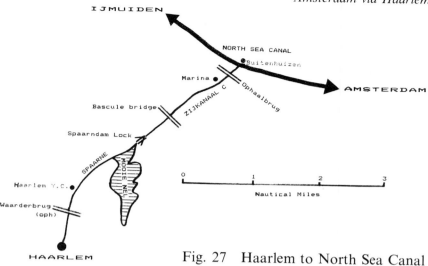

Fig. 27   Haarlem to North Sea Canal

three times a day Mon–Sat, and once on Sundays. From Sassenheim to Haarlem, Sunday opening is restricted to once or twice. From Haarlem to the Noordzee Kanaal, there are similar restrictions on Sundays. Furthermore, the central bridge across Zijkanaal C only opens thrice daily on any day of the week. Once through to the Noordzee Kanaal there are no more bridges or locks this side of Amsterdam.

ROUTE 3   Inland from Den Helder

ANWB charts F, Alkmaar—Den Helder; and G, Amsterdam—Alkmaar
This section deals with the two inland routes from Den Helder to Amsterdam via the North Sea Canal. It is also possible to go from Den Helder via the IJsselmeer, by taking the short sea passage from Den Helder to Den Oever and locking into the IJsselmeer there *(fig. 16)*, whereupon the passage becomes Route 5, IJsselmeer to Amsterdam.

The two inland routes from Den Helder go 21 miles via the Noordhollands Kanaal S to Alkmaar *(fig. 28)*. From there, one route is via the Nauernase Vaart and Zijkanaal D to the Noordzee Kanaal; while the other goes via the River Zaan and Zijkanaal G to the Noordzee Kanaal *(fig. 30)*.

Den Helder

Sea passages to Den Helder are covered in pilot books and by chart book 1801 *(Noordzeekust, Oostende tot Den Helder)*. The harbour is best shown by the inset on sheet 1801.8. Entry is possible at any state of tide, but if in doubt call up Harbour Control on VHF channel 14. The yacht harbour is the first inlet on the starboard side after entering harbour and passing the control tower. It is run by the Royal Netherlands Navy and has pontoon berths with water hoses, and a diesel pump outside the harbourmaster's office. Customs clearance is provided at the same office. Shower and toilet facilities are in the basement of the officers' club by the yacht harbour.

It is about 20 minutes' walk to the town centre which has a very good shopping precinct. There are sailmakers, engine repairers, boatyards, ANWB office; and a launderette and chandlery on the W side of the Binnenhaven.

In 1799 the Duke of York landed here with a force of 10,000 English troops and 13,000 Russians, but was defeated by French and Dutch forces. In 1811 the town was fortified by Napoleon, and has since become the chief Dutch naval base and training centre. There is a fine maritime museum which exhibits the history of the Dutch Royal Navy since 1813.

Den Helder to Alkmaar

ANWB chart F: Alkmaar—Den Helder

This first part of the inland route from Den Helder to Amsterdam goes via the Noordhollands Kanaal to the Alkmaardermeer, a lake just S of Alkmaar. From the yacht harbour by the officers' club, proceed into the Nieuwe Diep through the Vice-Admiral Moormanbrug. This bridge opens at all times but there are delays during rush hour traffic. Use VHF channel 18 if you wish to contact the bridge keeper. Continue to the lock at the N end of the Noordhollands Kanaal, the Koopvaardersschutsluis, entered through a bascule bridge; it opens at all times and uses VHF channel 22. There is a mooring stage at its entrance into the Noordhollands Kanaal. Once through the lock there is a series of marinas on the E side of the Binnenhaven; these have showers and fuel. There is another marina with similar facilities on the opposite side in the Industriehaven, but this entails entry though the Burg. Visserbrug, opening: Mon–Fri 5–23h; Sat 7–13, 14–19h; Sun, hols 7.30–12.30, 14.30–21h.

From the Koopvaardersschutsluis *(fig. 28)* proceed S down the Noordhollands Kanaal for 2 miles. A branch off to the SE should be ignored; just S of this junction pass through the De Kooy *ophaalbrug*. This opens: Mon–Fri 5–23h; Sat 7–13h, 14–19h; Sun, hols 9–13, 14–19h. There are delays during rush hours.

Half a mile further on, a railway bridge at Koegras opens half-hourly. The bridge keeper lowers a clog to passing yachts (a guilder donation should suffice). On the S side of this bridge, a roadside filling station on the W bank of the canal also has a mooring stage with diesel. After another mile beware of the *pontveer* at Noorderhaven: a ferry which effectively blocks the canal as it is attached by cable to both banks. Unless you are prepared for this, you could quite easily not notice the cables. So wait for the ferryman to lower the cable when he is ready for you to pass through.

Continue from the *pontveer* another 3 miles to the *pontonbrug* at 't Zand. This type of bridge *(fig. 2)*, also called a *vlotbrug*, is not seen on any of the other routes to Amsterdam. It opens at the same times as the De Kooy bridge. There is a mooring stage on the N side of the bridge at the W bank. The next bridge is nearly 2 miles away at Stolpen and opens at the same times as the De Kooy bridge, except for Sundays and holidays: 10–13, 15–18h.

The next two bridges are *vlotbruggen* which opens at the same times as de Kooy. At Sint Maartensvlotbrug, 2 miles S of Stolpen, there is a bakery on the N side of the bridge at the W bank and mooring is possible at the E bank. At Burgervlotbrug it is possible to moor to the bank on either side of this bridge. This stretch of the canal passes only a mile inland from the North Sea, which

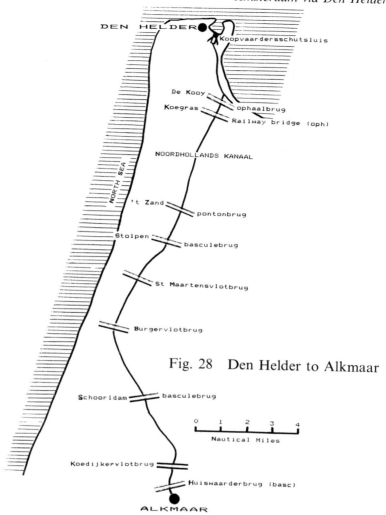

DEN HELDER

Koopvaardersschutsluis

De Kooy

Koegras

ophaalbrug

Railway bridge (oph)

NOORDHOLLANDS KANAAL

NORTH SEA

't Zand

pontonbrug

Stolpen

basculebrug

St Maartensvlotbrug

Burgervlotbrug

Fig. 28   Den Helder to Alkmaar

Schoorldam

basculebrug

```
0    1    2    3    4
Nautical Miles
```

Koedijkervlotbrug

Huiswaarderbrug (basc)

ALKMAAR

can be seen by standing on a high part of the boat.

Beyond Burgervlotbrug the canal turns inland again and it is possible to moor to the banks at Zijpersluis, a mile away. Schoorldam bridge opens at the same times as before. Here the scenery is noticeably different, with high wooded sand dunes between the canal and the North Sea.

The Koedijkervlotbrug 3 miles away also opens at the same times as the De Kooy bridge. This is quite a pretty area as many of the houses on the Koedijk waterfront have thatched roofs, and there is an attractive windmill on the S side of the bridge with wooded sandhills to the W. In fact the whole of the Noordhollands Kanaal between Den Helder and Alkmaar is very pleasant. It is wide and rural with an abundance of great crested grebes and ducks; and there are plenty of places between villages where it is possible to moor to the banks, although mooring spikes are advisable.

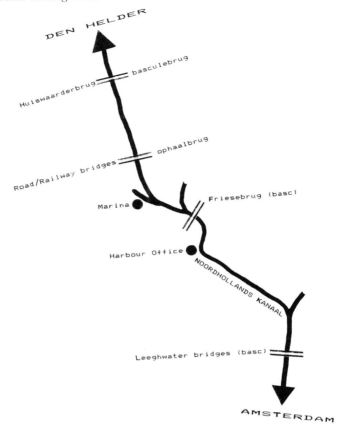

Fig. 29   Alkmaar

The Huiswaarderbrug on the outskirts of Alkmaar is a mile from the previous bridge and opens at the same times as the bridge at Stolpen. Next, after another half mile, is a combined road and rail *ophaalbrug (fig. 29)*. It opens daily, twice an hour. Just S of this bridge, on the W bank, a small inlet called the Afgesneden Kanaalvak houses the compact Alkmaar town marina. It has box moorings but no facilities; however, it is only 5 minutes from a supermarket and 10 from the town centre. If that is too far to walk, proceed through the next bridge, the bascule Friesebrug. Opening times are: Mon–Fri 5–7.45, 8.45–16.10, 17.10–23h; Sat 7–13, 14–19h; Sun, hols 10–13, 15–18h. The S bank of the Noordhollands Kanaal on the E side of this bridge, the Bierkade, is a public mooring quay where yachts can stay while visiting the town. The harbourmaster's office is situated here and contains showers and toilets; its mooring stage has a water hose, for which there is a small charge. Overnight mooring and shower fees are paid at the office, which issues an excellent town plan with all the most useful facilities marked. The Bierkade is only 5 minutes from the town centre, and has a well stocked chandlery and a take-away snack bar. Unfortunately it is rather noisy from the traffic, and seems to be a favourite walk for dog owners judging by the fouling of one's mooring lines and footwear. The town marina is much quieter and cleaner.

100

Alkmaar

The town was founded in the 12th century but the most important year in its history is 1573 when the Spaniards were forced to abandon their siege. This victory was to be the turning point in the Dutch struggle for independence. The lovely old town is small enough to be thoroughly explored without getting footsore. Its canals are crossed by quaint white wooden bridges and bordered with picturesque old houses. The most prominent building is the Waaggebouw or weighhouse, formerly a 14th century chapel. It stands in a square where the cheese market is held every Friday morning, still in the same fashion and dress as it was 300 years ago. At noon, when trading ceases, the weighhouse belfry chimes and displays a troop of lancers riding from the clock tower. Other notable buildings are the town hall and St Laurenskerk. The shopping centre is compact and well stocked and there are sailmakers, engine repairers, boatyards, ANWB office and a launderette.

Alkmaar to Amsterdam

ANWB chart G: Amsterdam—Alkmaar
From the Friesebrug continue along the Noordhollands Kanaal for a mile to the Leeghwaterbrug. This dual bascule bridge opens: Mon–Fri 5–16.30, 17.30–23h; Sat 7–13, 14–19h; Sun, hols 10–13, 15–18h. Continuing S for another 3 miles, the canal enters a large lake called the Alkmaardermeer *(fig. 30)*. But just before this, beware of the ferry crossing N of Akersloot. This is a *pontveer* with cables right across the canal: again, wait for the ferryman to lower them.

Alkmaardermeer

The lake offers a choice of routes, and a selection of marinas with all facilities, but outside the buoyed channel, depths are less than 2 m. The direction of buoyage is from N to S. Akersloot at its N entrance and Uitgeest at the SW corner are the main sailing centres; De Woude on the E side caters for power boats.

The route from Alkmaar to Amsterdam leaves the Noordhollands Kanaal at the NE corner of the lake. From here, our route continues S along the Markervaart to West Knollendam. The choice of routes through the lake is self-evident from ANWB chart G. One can take the Noordhollands Kanaal along the N side of the lake as far as, but not through, the Kogerpolderbrug and then turn S into the Markervaart. Alternatively, sail across the lake and into the Markervaart N or S of the De Woude promontory. There are mooring stages in the lake on the island of Nes and at the entrance to the Markervaart just S of Woudhaven. In the Markervaart itself the whole of the E bank between Stierop and De Woude is available for mooring. There is a café/restaurant on the W bank at De Woude with mooring places for customers.

The S end of the Markervaart at West Knollendam forms a T-junction with the Tapsloot. At this point the passage from Den Helder to Amsterdam proceeds to the Noordzee Kanaal by two alternative routes *(fig. 30)*: first, via the Nauernase Vaart and Zijkanaal D; second, via the River Zaan and Zijkanaal G.

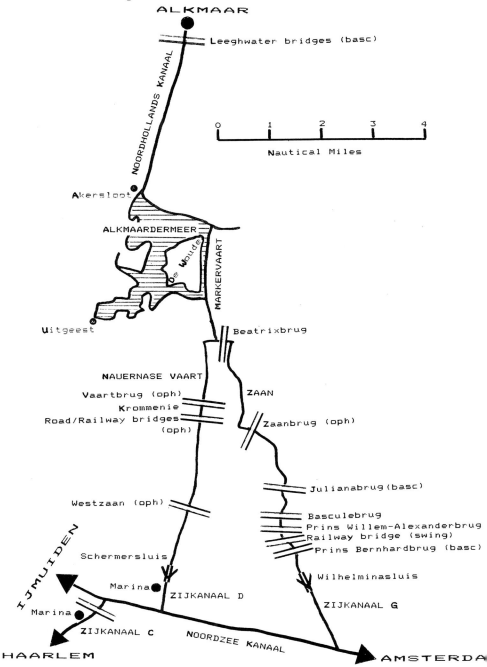

Fig. 30   Alkmaar to North Sea Canal

The Nauernase Vaart route has 5 bridges and a lock and reaches the Noordzee Kanaal about halfway between IJmuiden and Amsterdam. The River Zaan route has 9 bridges and a lock, but enters the Noordzee Kanaal much nearer Amsterdam. If your actual destination is Amsterdam, then the Zaan is better; but if your intention is to proceed via the Noordzee Kanaal to IJmuiden, or inland via Haarlem, then the Nauernase Vaart would be quicker.

Nauernase Vaart to the Noordzee Kanaal

This stage is 6 miles long. The S end of the Markervaart enters the Tapsloot: turn W at this point, towards an attractive windmill, and then S into the Nauernase Vaart. For the next mile there are mooring places on the E bank between the windmill and the first of three bridges at Krommenie.

The first of these, the Vaartbrug, opens: Mon–Fri 9.30–16.30 (Fri to 20h); Sat, Sun, hols 9–12, 14–18h. The next two are road and rail *ophaal* bridges which open half-hourly at the same times as the Vaartbrug. The bridge at Westzaan opens: Mon–Fri 8.30–16.30; Sat, Sun, hols closed. Moor to the bank while waiting.

Just over a mile S of the Westzaan bridge, the Nauernase Vaart ends at Nauerna at the Schermersluis lock, which works daily 9–12, 13–17, 18–20h (19h on Sat, Sun, hols). A fee is payable in the lock before passing through the *ophaalbrug* at its S end. There are mooring stages at each end of the lock. All the bridges from Krommenie to the lock are opened by the same man who travels from one to another by motor cycle.

The Schermersluis opens into Zijkanaal D which leads after half a mile into the Noordzee Kanaal by km 12. There is a marina at Nauerna on the W side of Zijkanaal D with box moorings, fuel pumps and showers, and it is a convenient place to stay before or after making a North Sea passage via IJmuiden. At km 12 where Zijkanaal D enters the Noordzee Kanaal, it is 7 miles to Amsterdam, 6 miles to IJmuiden, or 1 mile to Zijkanaal C and the route to Haarlem.

River Zaan to the Noordzee Kanaal

This alternative route is 7 miles. From Alkmaar and the Alkmaardermeer proceed into the Markervaart, which ends at the Tapsloot where the westbound arm goes to the Nauernase Vaart. The eastbound arm of the Tapsloot ends almost immediately at the Beatrixbrug, which opens on the half and whole hour: Mon–Fri 6.30–21h; Sat 7.30–12, 13–19h; Sun, hols 8–12, 15–19h. From the bridge turn S into the River Zaan, where there are three marinas on the W bank. The direction of buoyage in the river is from N to S.

The next bridge is almost 2 miles on at Wormerveer, the Zaanbrug, opening: Mon–Fri 6–21h; Sat 7.30–12, 13–17.45h; Sun, hols 8.30–10, 16–19h. On the W side of the bridge moor at the S bank, for shopping. Just over a mile on, the next town is Zaandijk with the bascule Julianabrug. Opening times are: Mon–Fri 6.15–21h; Sat 7.30–12, 13–17.15h; Sun, hols 8.30–10, 16–19h. Zaandijk has a very picturesque waterfront with green wooden houses on both sides and a line *(gang)* of five windmills on the E bank.

The next two bridges are bascule bridges at Koog a.d. Zaan, $\frac{1}{2}$ mile from

Zaandijk. The northernmost is the bridge carrying the Coentunnelweg, opening: Mon–Fri 6.15–7.30, 8.30–12, 13–17, 18–21h; Sat 7.30–12, 13–16.45h; Sun, hols 8.30–9.30, 17–19h. The second is the Prins Willem-Alexanderbrug, open: Mon–Fri 6.15–21h; Sat 7.30–12, 13–16.45h; Sun, hols 8.15–10.30, 16.30–19h. There is a windmill museum at Koog a.d. Zaan, housed in an old mill which dates back to 1751.

The next bridge is a quarter of a mile away and the first of four at Zaandam. It is a railway swing bridge which opens at the same times as the Prins Willem-Alexanderbrug. There is a yacht mooring stage on its N side at the W bank, by a block of flats with its own private marina occupying the 'ground floor'. The second bridge, the Prins Bernhardbrug, opens at the same times as the Prins Willem-Alexanderbrug. In the 17th century, Zaandam was the world's leading shipbuilding centre. Peter the Great studied shipbuilding techniques here, and there is a statue of him in the market place.

The last two bridges at Zaandam are bascule bridges at each end of the Wilhelminasluis. The N one is the Prinses Beatrixbrug and the S the Wilhelminabrug. The bridges and lock use VHF channel 20 and open: Mon–Fri 6–21.45h; Sat 7.30–12, 13–18h; Sun, hols 8–10.30, 16–19h. The lock forms a barrier between the fresh water of the River Zaan and salt water of Zijkanaal G. A fee for passage of the Zaan is payable at the office on the E side of the lock. The W side has a low wall which makes it easy to tie up inside the lock. There is a mooring place on the S side of the Wilhelminabrug at the E bank.

The Wilhelminasluis opens into Zijkanaal G, which in turn joins the Noordzee Kanaal just over a mile S of the lock and 3 miles W of Amsterdam. There are marinas on each side of Zijkanaal G. Passage of the Noordzee Kanaal is now covered in Route 4, IJmuiden to Amsterdam.

ROUTE 4 IJmuiden to Amsterdam

ANWB chart G: Amsterdam—Alkmaar

A direct passage across the North Sea to IJmuiden and up the Noordszee Kanaal is the quickest way of getting from the E coast of England to Amsterdam. The entrance to IJmuiden is well covered in the North Sea pilot books, so there is little that need be said here. If your passage to IJmuiden is along the Dutch coast rather than across the North Sea, then Dutch chart book 1801 *(Noordzeekust, Oostende tot Den Helder)* is the best one to use. Chart 1801.6 shows the approaches to IJmuiden, and the inset shows the harbour on a larger scale. It is easily recognized by its cluster of tall chimneys, which can be seen from far offshore. The entrance is protected by two long moles which give a large expanse of sheltered water. The inner harbour entrance has an island (Forteiland) which should be passed on its S side. This way leads to the small S lock (Zuidersluis), which is the one used by yachts and other small vessels going into the North Sea Canal. Ocean-going ships use the large locks on the N side of the island. If in doubt about entry, call up Harbour Control on VHF channel 12.

The Customs office is at the entrance to the Zuidersluis. If this is your first port of call in the Netherlands, tie up at their landing stage on the N bank and clear Customs and Immigration before entering the lock. The Immigration office is housed in a separate building: from the Customs office, walk across the swing bridge over the lock to the S bank; cross the road (Kanaaldijk), turn

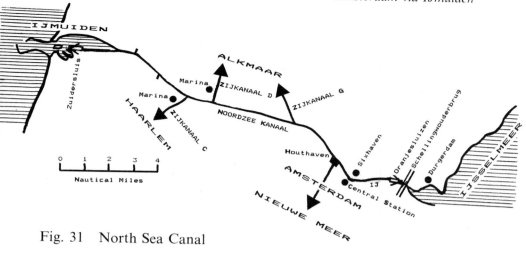

Fig. 31 North Sea Canal

left and walk as far as the end of the lock to no. 240, the office of the Koninklijke Marechaussee Nederland.

The lock is worked daily 6–21h. For passage into the Noordzee Kanaal outside these times, call up Harbour Control on VHF channel 12. The lock walls have rope loops which make easy work of attaching mooring lines.

Noordzee Kanaal

The canal is 13 miles long, from the IJmuiden locks to the centre of the Amsterdam waterfront, where it becomes continuous with the River IJ, *(fig. 31)*. It took 11 years to build and was opened in 1876. Before that time all of Amsterdam's sea trade had reached the city through the Zuiderzee, but as this became silted up a new route was needed. This led to construction of the Noordzee Kanaal which is wide, deep and straight and carries a great deal of traffic, including ocean-going vessels. It has no bridges or locks and its banks are marked with kilometre posts. Yachts are obliged to keep to the starboard bank.

After entering through the Zuidersluis at IJmuiden, there are mooring places on the S bank which are convenient for visiting the town. For an overnight stop there are two marinas in quiet sheltered inlets just off the main canal. The first is on the S side of the Noordzee Kanaal, in Zijkanaal C which is 5 miles from IJmuiden by km 10. This is the IJmond marina which was described in the section on Route 2, Haarlem to Amsterdam (page 96). The next marina is another mile farther on by km 12, on the N side in Zijkanaal D at Nauerna (described under Route 3, page 103).

At km 18, 3 miles E of Zijkanaal D, the route from Alkmaar via the River Zaan enters the Noordzee Kanaal through Zijkanaal G; and just over 2 miles further E, on the S bank, is the Houthaven which is the end of the inland Route 1 to Amsterdam via the Nieuwe Meer. The Noordzee Kanaal ends a mile E of the Houthaven, by Amsterdam Central Station, and the waterway continues E as the River IJ into the IJsselmeer.

ROUTE 5   IJsselmeer to Amsterdam

Chart 1810.2 and ANWB chart G

All routes from the IJsselmeer converge on its SW corner which is continuous with the E end of the River IJ. This joins the North Sea Canal at Amsterdam *(fig. 31)*.

From the IJsselmeer the buoyed Pampus channel leads to the E end of the IJ which is called the Buiten IJ (Outer IJ) (chart 1810.2 inset). Its S side has a stone wall and the N side has a channel off to a marina at Durgerdam. The Buiten IJ narrows and continues under the opening Schellingwouderbrug and then through a lock complex, the Oranjesluizen, where it becomes the Afgesloten IJ and forms the Amsterdam waterfront. From the IJsselmeer through the Buiten IJ to the locks, the direction of buoyage is that of the IJsselmeer—i.e. E to W—but in the Afgesloten IJ the direction of buoyage is that of the Noordzee Kanaal, from W to E.

Durgerdam

The entrance channel to 'Het IJ' marina at Durgerdam is well marked with port and starboard posts and is shown on chart 1810.2 insets. It has box moorings with electric points and water hoses; and a small clubhouse with toilets, showers (coin) and a public telephone. This marina is a convenient place to stay if Amsterdam is too crowded, or if you arrive in the Buiten IJ too late in the day to continue W to Amsterdam or E into the IJsselmeer. If the marina is full there is an anchorage on either side of the entrance channel which is sheltered from the N.

Durgerdam is about 4 miles from Amsterdam and there is a bus service from a stop opposite the marina entrance. The village is small and quaint and has no shops; it seems to consist of one road with just a restaurant and cafés, plus a bar with stocks outside.

Durgerdam to Amsterdam

The Schellingwouderbrug bascule bridge crosses the river just over a mile W of Durgerdam. It has mooring stages on both sides, and opens: Mon–Fri 6–7, 9–16, 18–22h; Sat 6–24h; Sn, hols 0–2.30, 9–21h. Almost immediately W of the bridge, the Buiten IJ is separated from the Afgesloten IJ by the Oranjesluizen complex which prevents salt water from the Noordzee Kanaal entering the fresh water IJsselmeer. The three locks open at all hours. There are mooring stages at both ends and the locks have a water tap and telephone booths. The bridge and locks use VHF channel 18. Between the bridge and locks a small marina on the N bank has box moorings and is called the W.V. 'Zuiderzee'.

Once through the locks, remember that the direction of buoyage changes. It is just 2 miles from the locks to Amsterdam city centre which is on the S bank of the IJ. Jachthaven Twellegea on the N bank, at the end of Zijkanaal K and just half a mile west of the Oranjesluizen, has box moorings, showers, diesel, clubhouse, boatyard, a small chandlery and a Volvo service agent. Situated in the suburb of Nieuwendam, it has a few shops opposite and is only a short bus ride from the city. Bus no. 32 goes direct to Amsterdam Central Station. The stop is on the main road just two minutes from the marina.

Durgerdam: Het Ij marina berths and clubhouse to the left. Village main street and bus stop for Amsterdam to right.

Half a mile further W there is a smaller marina on the N bank, at the end of the E section of the Johan van Hasseltkanaal. This one is called the Jachthaven Aeolus and has box moorings with water hoses; but no showers or other facilities.

Amsterdam

ANWB charts G, H

For information on where to go and what to see in Amsterdam visit the vvv office opposite the main entrance to the Central Station. The public transport enquiry office, bus and tram terminus are also situated here, as are the departure points for some excellent boat trips through the city canals.

There is a small yacht harbour known as the Spoorweghaven on the S bank of the IJ at the W end of the Central Station. It cannot be recommended, as it has no facilities and is exposed to constant road traffic noise and wash from barges. Its unique roadside position at a busy city station presents a real security risk if a boat is left unattended.

The best and most convenient marina in Amsterdam is in the Sixhaven, on the N bank of the IJ opposite the Central Station. It can easily be found by watching for the large ferry which crosses the river to and from the Station. The entrance to the Sixhaven is the second inlet to the E of the ferry terminus. Set in pleasant wooded surroundings, the marina has box moorings and a nice clubhouse with showers (tokens from the harbourmaster). There is no charge for use of electricity and water hoses at the moorings. Drinking and boat cleaning water are supplied in separate hoses: the narrow hose has drinking water and the wider one is for washing the boat—not for drinking as it comes direct from the river.

The ferry to Amsterdam is only five minutes' walk from the marina: leave by the clubhouse exit, cross the lock in the Noordhollands Kanaal, and turn left at the road. It operates day and night and is free. From the S bank ferry terminus, cross the road and walk through the back entrance of the Central

Station to reach all the tourist facilities outside the front entrance.

Although Amsterdam has an excellent shopping centre, not too far from the Central Station, it is quicker to stay on the Sixhaven side of the river for food stores. Leave the Sixhaven by the car park exit and walk along the right side of Meeuwenlaan to the Motorkade (10–15 minutes) where a large supermarket caters for all needs. As in Alkmaar, a deposit is necessary for use of a trolley. A new supermarket is under construction much nearer the marina, on the same side of Meeuwenlaan. Halfway between the Sixhaven and the Motorkade, but on the opposite side of the road, the street called Valkenweg has a bank and a bakery on its Meeuwenlaan corner. Turn into Valkenweg for a small shopping centre which includes a post office, butcher, baker, and a snack bar that provides take-away chips and spit-roasted chickens. Return from these shops to the Sixhaven by a choice of three different routes: the way you came, via Nachtegaalstraat, or along the towpath of the Noordhollands Kanaal. If you have acquired a little knowledge of Dutch, you will notice that all the streets on the N side of Meeuwenlaan are named after birds.

(left) Amsterdam: Oranjesluizen as seen from city centre heading towards Ijsselmeer. Span of Schellingwouderbrug beyond right-hand lock.

Amsterdam: entrance to Sixhaven yacht harbour. Note Shell building in background on west side of harbour. This is a useful landmark for finding the Sixhaven.

CHAPTER 10

The IJsselmeer and the Zuiderzee Project

Chart 1810: IJsselmeer met Randmeren
The IJsselmeer (Lake IJssel) did not exist before 1932, and the Randmeren (peripheral lakes) only came into existence during the period 1942–68. At the time of the Roman Empire the area now covered by chart 1810 contained many fresh water lakes, including a large one called Lake Flevo. During the following centuries coastal erosion led to the sea breaking into these lakes, and by 1200 the area was transformed into a large bay which was a southern extension of the North Sea. It was accordingly called the Zuiderzee (Southern Sea), and so it remained until 1932 when it was sealed off from the North Sea by the 16 mile long Afsluitdijk (Barrier Dam).

An understanding of the transformation of the Zuiderzee *(fig. 32)* into the IJsselmeer, and its subsequent development *(fig. 33)*, will make a visit to this area much more interesting. The Zuiderzee Project is accordingly described now, and the cruising grounds later.

The Zuiderzee Project

Reclamation of the Zuiderzee had been a dream of the Dutch nation for centuries, and in 1667 the first practical scheme was devised by Hendrik Stevin. His plan was to build dams between the mainland and the Frisian Islands and thereby seal off the Zuiderzee, but it was too big an undertaking to be feasible at that time. It was not until 1891 that Dr Lely produced a plan which was compatible with current technology and resources. The idea was to seal off the Zuiderzee from the Waddenzee by constructing a dam across its mouth and then to reclaim large tracts of land from the resultant lake. Work began in 1920 and the Afsluitdijk was completed in 1932, but Dr Lely did not live to see his new lake as he died in 1929. The new saline lake was called the IJsselmeer as it was fed with fresh water from the River IJssel. This river is a branch of the Rhine and its flow of fresh water from the Swiss mountains formerly went to waste in the Zuiderzee.

The reason for transforming the Zuiderzee into a lake was primarily to prevent flooding, but it had several other important results. First, the inflow from the River IJssel led to its desalination and gave rise to the fresh water *meer* which provides this part of the Netherlands with an ample water supply. Also, land was reclaimed from the IJsselmeer to form large polders, which provided more agricultural land, space for building new towns to accomodate overspill from crowded inland cities, and land for creating forests, nature

Fig. 32   Zuiderzee—1730

reserves and leisure areas. Large-scale reclamation to form polders required modern technology and sufficient resources, but the basic principles have been known for centuries. An area of water is enclosed by building a wall around it, and the water is pumped out. The reclaimed land is cultivated while the surrounding wall prevents further flooding.

Before the Afsluitdijk was completed, work had already begun on reclamation of the NW corner of the Zuiderzee by building a dam in the open sea between Den Oever, on the island of Wieringen, and Medemblik. It created the first sea water lake and by 1930 this had been drained to form the Wieringermeerpolder. But the former seabed was so saturated with salt that it took another year's work before it could be cultivated.

The next part of Dr Lely's plan to reclaim the IJsselmeer began in 1936 with the building of another offshore dam on its eastern side. This was completed in 1940, but by then the IJsselmeer had already become a fresh water lake; so when the new enclosed area was pumped dry in 1942 it was possible to grow crops without delay. The new polder was called the Noordoost Polder (Northeast Polder) and extends from Lemmer to Urk *(fig. 33)*. Urk was once an island, 15 miles offshore *(fig. 32)*. The polder also enclosed the former island of Schokland which contains the settlements of Ens and Emmeloord *(figs. 32 & 33)*.

The last polder to be created was Flevoland at the SE corner of the IJsselmeer. It was reclaimed in two stages as eastern and southern Flevoland, but they form one continuous polder. The enclosing dam for eastern Flevoland was completed in 1956 and a year later it was pumped dry to form Oostelijk Flevoland (East Flevoland polder). The dam for the southern part

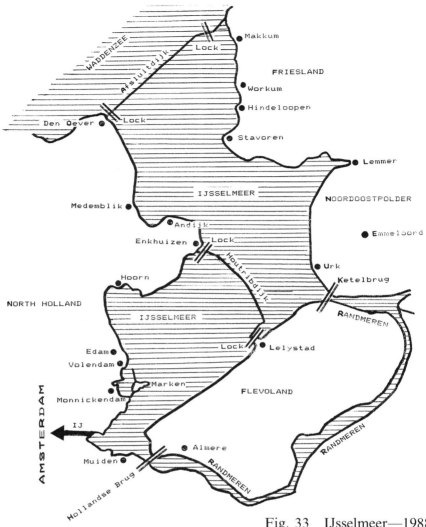

Fig. 33   IJsselmeer—1988

was started in 1959 and finished in 1967. A year later the area was drained to form Zuidelijk Flevoland. Meanwhile, in 1967 a new town called Lelystad was created in East Flevoland. Similarly, in 1976 the first stage of a new town called Almere was built in South Flevoland.

The outstanding difference between Flevoland and the other IJsselmeer polders is that the latter were created in continuity with the original coastline of the Zuiderzee, whereas Flevoland was so constructed as to leave a series of narrow lakes between the polders and the original shoreline. These were called Randmeren *(fig. 33)* or peripheral lakes. A number of old Zuiderzee fishing ports are now on the mainland shores of the Randmeren, while a series of brand-new towns and villages face them from the opposite side. (The Randmeren are described in the next chapter.)

The final part of Dr Lely's plan was the creation of one more polder called Markerwaard, which was to occupy the SW part of the IJsselmeer opposite Flevoland. The Houtribdijk was completed in 1975, between Enkhuizen and Lelystad: it divides the IJsselmeer into separate northern and southern parts though there is access between them through locks at each end of the dam. It was to be the northern limit of the Markerwaard polder, but this part of the project is controversial and it is not yet certain whether it will be continued. Opposition is centred on environmental and financial issues. The government has approved its completion in principle but it has been left for public opinion to make the final decision.

The whole story of the Zuiderzee Project can be seen at the Nieuw Land exhibition at Lelystad (see page 116).

Passage Planning

Chart 1810.1 *(fig. 33)* gives an overall view of the area. It will be seen that the IJsselmeer is accessible from the sea through locks at each end of the Afsluitdijk; and the Houtribdijk also has locks at each end to allow shipping to pass between Amsterdam and the N part of the IJsselmeer. The polders and Randmeren are shown in the SE. The chart also shows how well the area is covered by RDF beacons and fog signals; and sets yet another example of excellence by including the call signs, Morse identity and frequencies of radio beacons.

Chart 1810.2 *IJsselmeer—Zuidelijk Gedeelte* covers the southern part and the direction of buoyage is towards Amsterdam. There are four points of entry to the area:

1. From Amsterdam through the locks in the River IJ (Oranjesluizen), as described in the previous chapter.
2. From the Randmeren beneath the fixed Hollandse Brug, described in the next chapter.
3, 4. Through the locks at each end of the Houtribdijk. The Enkhuizen entrance is on chart 1810.3.

Durgerdam, one of the Amsterdam marinas already described in Chapter 9, is well shown on this chart and its insets. However, Edam, Volendam, Monnickendam and Marken are on the Gouwzee chart 1810.6, and are accordingly described later under that chart.

Muiden

Situated at the S end of the IJsselmeer, Muiden is entered through a well marked channel shown on the chart 1810.2 inset. The River Vecht flows into the IJsselmeer at the S end of this channel; there is a fort and cannon on its W bank and Muiden castle (Muiderslot) on the E side. On the W bank, between the fort and the castle, visiting yachts are welcome to stay at the Royal Netherlands Sailing and Rowing Club (K.N.Z. & R.V). This has box moorings with water hoses and electricity, and there is a diesel pump on the reception stage. As its title suggests, this is a very well appointed yacht harbour with uniformed staff and excellent toilet and (coin) shower facilities. There is a boatyard (Moody agent) and chandlery next door.

On the opposite side of the river, immediately S of the castle, Jachthaven Stichting has similar facilities but is not as spacious or luxurious; there is a sailmaker close by. A little farther upriver is the Zeesluis and it is possible to moor at the E bank, just N of the space reserved for craft awaiting entry. This lock was built in 1694 but has been restored and now has a swing bridge across its S end. Rope loops along its walls make it easy to attach mooring warps. Opening times are: Mon–Fri 7.30–11.30, 12.15–13, 13.30–21h; Sat, Sun, hols 7.30–21h. Beyond the lock there are mooring places along the Herengracht on the E bank of the Vecht, and along the Vechtkade on its W bank. Next comes a bascule bridge but there is no point in passing through unless you are prepared to lower your mast farther upriver. There is a small marina on its N side called the Jachthaven Van Deursen, with box moorings, toilets and (coin) showers.

Muiden has a small but adequate selection of shops and is usually crowded with tourists. The main attraction is its impressive castle, the Muiderslot. This is surrounded by a moat full of sizeable fish and is well worth a visit. The castle was built in 1280, but after some bloodthirsty events typical of the times it was razed to the ground. It was rebuilt in its present form in 1370 and subsequently underwent a complete change of character, becoming a seat of culture and playing host to writers, poets, scholars and artists. This peaceful role has continued ever since.

Hoorn

As shown on the chart inset, there is a choice of three mooring places at Hoorn. The Grashaven, at the port side of the harbour entrance, contains a marina 'De Nieuwe Haven' with all facilities and a launderette. The next marina, 'W.V. de Hoorn', is in the *vluchthaven* opposite the Hoofdtoren harbour defence tower and set inside the pleasant surroundings of the Julianapark. It has box moorings and all facilities. If you do not require full marina facilities, moor to the quayside in the inner harbour (Binnenhaven). This is cheaper and more crowded but has a toilet/shower block. Alternatively, if you have a dinghy, there is a sheltered anchorage 2 m deep in the Buitenhaven (outer harbour), E of the yellow buoys.

One of the best preserved towns in the Netherlands, Hoorn was once an important trading port on the Zuiderzee. In 1573, within sight of the town, local warships defeated a Spanish fleet and captured its admiral. In 1616 a local citizen became the first person to sail his ship round the S tip of South America; hence the name Cape Horn in honour of his home town. Hoorn was at the height of its prosperity in the heyday of the East Indies Company, but gradually declined in importance as the Zuiderzee silted up and became too shallow for ocean-going ships. The main square contains the 1609 public weighbridge (Waag) and the 1631 West Friesland museum. Hoorn is a very good shopping centre and has an excellent market every Wednesday. There is a steam museum and a steam train service to Medemblik.

Lelystad

The dam between Enkhuizen and Lelystad has locks at each end, and those at Lelystad, the Houtribsluizen, have good mooring facilities on each side. There is a bascule bridge across the lock complex and a yellow flashing light indicates which lock to enter. They open at all times and listen on VHF channel 20. A wall continues S from the dam for another 2 miles past the locks, but it has a small opening at their S exit for yachts crossing the IJsselmeer. A very high

(above) Hoorn: approaching harbour from Ijseelmeer, showing Hoofdtoren in the centre. WV De Hoorn marina off picture to the right.

Hoorn: Binnenhaven looking towards entrance and top of Hoofdtoren boats moored alongside on either side.

post office tower (140 m) by the locks makes an excellent landmark.

The W.V. Lelystad marina is situated in the Houtribhaven at the N side of the locks. On arrival tie up at the reception stage (signposted *Meldsteiger*) and take a marina plan from the green box by the intercom. Then use the latter to report your arrival to the Harbourmaster, who will direct you to one of the berths marked on the plan. Visitors are usually directed to the Passantenkom, where you tie up alongside long stages. There are water hoses, electricity, (coin) showers, launderette, diesel pump and lifting-out crane, and a small food shop that is open on Sundays. The key to the laundry room is obtainable from the HM for a charge. (The machine is very small, so take a good book if you have a lot of washing.)

'Marina Lelystad' is at Houtribhoek, about 2 miles N of the locks. It has box moorings and all facilities but is a long way from town.

Lelystad is the main centre of population in East Flevoland. It is a new town, built on land which was once the bottom of the Zuiderzee, and did not exist before 1967. It was named after the Dutch engineer Lely who had masterminded the creation of the IJsselmeer and its polders, and was specially planned to provide a better quality of life for its inhabitants. With traffic-free residential, shopping and recreation areas, and enough industry to prevent it becoming a dormitory town, everything has been carefully sited to create the best possible environment. There are no high-rise flats; pedestrian, cycle and motor traffic are completely segregated; shopping and urban amenities are conveniently near residential areas; industry is confined to the outskirts and is served by a road system which avoids long journeys to work. Recreation areas, nature reserves and water sports centres are available in and around the town. The centre is an hour's walk from the marina but only 10 minutes by bus (the stop is by the lock). There is a very large shopping precinct with a vvv office, theatre, etc. Residential areas are beautifully laid out around the town centre.

Together with rebuilt Rotterdam, Lelystad makes a complete change from the ancient Dutch ports. It has none of their old-world charm or medieval atmosphere, yet it drives home with equal force the energy, dedication, foresight and engineering brilliance which have enabled the Dutch to win their centuries-long battle against the sea. Its culmination in the creation of the IJsselmeer and the polders is excellently displayed in the Nieuw Land exhibition on the S side of the locks, just 10 minutes' walk from the marina. All the exhibits are described in English as well as Dutch.

The Gouwzee

The S IJsselmeer is very shallow with maximum soundings of less than 5 m. The SW part opposite Lelystad is called the Gouwzee (chart 1810.6) and is even shallower with only 2.2 m in the buoyed channels, and outside them most of the charted soundings are little more than 1 m. Furthermore the chart shows another hazard just outside these channels: *waterplanten*, in red ink. These dense beds of weed quickly render a propeller ineffective, so be warned and keep to the buoyed channels. The Gouwzee contains the old fishing ports of Marken, Monnickendam, Volendam and Edam.

Marken

After the great flood of 1164 Marken became an island, and remained so until 1957 when it was joined to the mainland by a causeway. A wall has also been built from the N tip of the island, stretching for over a mile NNW as far as the 2 m contour. The chart also shows an underwater wall *(berm)* between Jan Hagelhoek on the mainland and the N part of Marken. It has an opening for the buoyed channel. These walls are preparations for the Markerwaard polder reclamation. The E tip of Marken has a prominent white lighthouse where the channel from Amsterdam to Hoorn passes close to the island. The causeway prevents any such through passage on the Gouwzee side W of Marken.

Marken habour, on the Gouwzee, is divided into three sections, the Oude, Nieuwe and West Haven; yachts can moor in any one of them, though none have any toilets or showers. The town is attractive with dark green, quaint, wooden houses originally built on stilts to prevent flooding, though most have now been bricked in. Many of the older women still wear full traditional costume but the men have only retained their clogs. Large numbers of visitors arrive daily in the tourist boats from Volendam. The food shops are scattered among the narrow streets and have to be searched for.

Marken lighthouse: situated on Ijsselmeer side of Marken, as seen from Amsterdam to Hoorn channel.

Monnickendam

Here there is a good choice of marinas. Approach the harbour through the buoyed Monnickendammer Gat channel which has 2.2 m (outside this channel there is little more than 1 m). Before reaching the old town harbour there are four marinas, two of them to port and opposite each other in the same inlet: the 'Hemmeland' and 'Van Goor' marinas with box moorings and all facilities. Van Goor marina is a little nearer the town centre and has a chandlery and small restaurant. Just past these two marinas, on the starboard side of the channel, the 'Gouwzee' marina also has all facilities and a large clubhouse and restaurant. The other marina on the starboard side is the 'De Zeilhoek', the smallest and farthest from town. The nearest berths to the town centre are in the old town harbour: take the starboard entrance after passing Gouwzee marina. The berths belong to the W.V. 'Monnickendam'; there are toilets, showers, and fuel pumps.

Monnickendam means monks' dam. The town was founded by Frisian monks who built a small dam here in the 13th century. It is a picturesque town with a fine belfry *(speeltoren)* which displays marching knights while the carillon chimes. The 1660 Waag is a fine building which now houses a restaurant. The 15th century church tower, together with the *speeltoren*, gives Monnickendam an impressive skyline. Shopping is adequate and there is a launderette at 1 Kalversteeg.

Volendam: showing harbour entrance from quayside and local yacht berths to right of picture. Visitors moor off picture to the left.

Volendam

The Volendam end of the Gouwzee is a little deeper, with 2.4 m in the buoyed channel. There are no marina berths for visitors, and the harbour is crowded with fishing boats and the ferries to Marken. Visiting yachts moor to the quayside in the NE half of the harbour. There is a small toilet/shower block on the landward side of the harbour by its N end, and also a fuel barge at that end.

The harbour is an attractive sight when its fleet of fishing boats are unloading their catch, while an abundance of herons perch on mooring posts or the gunwales of the fishing boats. Although much commercialised, Volendam is a quaint little town with small wooden houses, a good selection of shops, and a museum. There are sailmakers and a marine diesel workshop.

Edam

The entrance canal to Edam has a very narrow opening into the IJsselmeer, so wait for outgoing craft to get clear before entering. The seaward end of the canal is called the Buitenhaven and yachts can moor to either bank; there is a water hose on the N bank. However it is much better to proceed right into town through the Zeesluis and *ophaalbrug* (Kettingbrug), open: Mon–Fri 8–13, 14–20h; Sat, Sun, hols 9–13, 14–19h. There are mooring stages at both ends of the lock and a charge is levied inside. On the E side of the manually

Edam: approaching Kettingbrug from Zeesluis. Yacht berths are through bridge alongside Nieuwe Haven on the right side.

operated Kettingbrug there is a sail loft and mast-lifting crane. Beyond the bridge there is a mooring stage on the S bank, reserved for waiting. The rest of the canal as far as the next bridge (Baanbrug) has mooring space on both banks: the N bank is called the Nieuwe Haven and the S is the Marken. There are no toilet or shower facilities but the Nieuwe Haven has a water hose just before the Baanbrug. It is the more convenient for visiting the town as it is only 2 minutes from the centre.

Edam is one of the loveliest and best preserved of all the Zuiderzee ports. At the height of its prosperity in the 16th and 17th centuries, it rivalled Amsterdam, Enkhuizen and Hoorn as a shipbuilding centre, but in common with them it went into decline as the Zuiderzee silted up. However, the lakes surrounding Edam were drained at that time and the reclaimed farmland allowed it to prosper anew as a leading cheese producer. Many of the buildings from those days remain, and the Captain's House (1530) is a beautiful building which now houses a fascinating museum and the famous floating cellar. But the whole town should be thoroughly explored, best done using the excellent town walking guide from the vvv.

Until 1922 Edam held a cheese market similar to that at Alkmaar, and the original Kaaswaag is still open for the sale of cheese. The town is a very good shopping centre, and a convenient chicken and chips take-away in Prinsenstraat is open until 2300.

Chart 1810.3: IJsselmeer—Noordelijk Gedeelte covers: the seaward half of the IJsselmeer between the Afsluitdijk at its N end and the Houtribdijk; the entrances from seaward and the passages to the S part of the IJsselmeer through the locks at Enkhuizen and Lelystad; entry to the Randmeren via the Ketelmeer; and access to the Friesland lakes via Makkum, Workum, Stavoren and Lemmer. The direction of buoyage is from the Afsluitdijk southwards.

Enkhuizen

Entry to Enkhuizen is through a deep channel called the Krabbersgat, separated by a wall from the 1 m depths over the Enkhuizerzand. Approaching from the S, a lock and opening bridge must first be negotiated. The lock complex is the Krabbersgatsluizen and listens on VHF channel 22. Opening times are Mon–Sat 03–23h; Sun, hols 08–20h. There are good mooring facilities on each side of the lock approaches.

On leaving the lock the first inlet to port is the Buyshaven. This has a marina on its S side and the railway station on the N. The marina has box moorings and a well-appointed toilet/shower block, but is the farthest from the town centre. The station side is reserved for tourist boats. The next entry is the Buitenhaven: this has yacht berths but gets very crowded, and you may have to moor alongside a trot of several boats. However, the Harbourmaster keeps everything under control from a small launch. There is a toilet/shower block adjacent to the office on the N side, where shower tokens are obtainable.

Continuing along the Krabbersgat, the last entrance is the Compagnieshaven which houses the largest marina. As you reach the entrance a loudspeaker asks (in English) how long you wish to stay. On replying in the direction of the loudspeaker, it then gives you a box number and precise instructions on where to find it. There is a launderette, showers (token), chandlery and fuel pumps; and water hoses at the moorings. It is just a short

*Enkhuizen: showing Drommedaris reference tower at the entrance to old town harbours.
(Not open to visiting yachts).*

walk from the marina to town.

This ancient walled town is yet another of the former Zuiderzee ports which
flourished in the Middle Ages. At the height of its prosperity it had a fleet of
400 North Sea fishing boats, but only the buildings and harbour remain as
records of its glorious past. Like Hoorn, the harbour entrance is dominated by
a defence tower called the Drommedaris (Dromedary) of 1540. Some of the
best preserved buildings are the Zuiderkerk, the Waag, and the Stadhuis. A
good walk along the ramparts will show the 1649 Koepoort, an old gate at the
W end of the town. Diametrically opposite this, at the E end of the ramparts
and close by the landward entrance to the Compagnieshaven, is the Staverse
Poortje (Stavoren Gate). There is a good shopping centre; also engine repairs,
boatyards and a sailmaker.

The transformation of the Zuiderzee into the IJsselmeer greatly changed the
lives of its inhabitants. Anxious to preserve a record of their life and times, the
Zuiderzee Museum was created in Enkhuizen and opened by the Queen in
1983. This superb exhibition, which should not be missed, is in two parts—
open air and indoors. The first (Buitenmuseum) is reached by a frequent boat
service from the station or the lock; it consists of a 130 house village of genuine
originals which were dismantled and rebuilt. The indoor museum
(Binnenmuseum) is housed in the 1625 Peperhuis almost opposite the

Enkhuizen: Buitenhaven, showing Drommedaris behind the harbour office. Harbour entrance to right of picture. Yacht berths off left of picture and off foreground.

Stavoren Gate. It contains a magnificent hall of original Zuiderzee sailing craft, and there are excellent displays of fishing techniques, household furniture and traditional dress.

Medemblik

A conspicuous white building just to the N of the town makes it easily recognised from seaward. The entrance to the harbour canal is very narrow and care must be taken not to strike submerged rocks on each side. This is most likely to happen if a large outgoing vessel occupies the middle and you try to get in by keeping over to one side. If anything large is coming out, wait until it is clear before making your own entry. The first part of the harbour, the Oosterhaven, is not available to visiting yachts. Next comes the Middenhaven, where yachts can lie alongside on either side of the harbour but there are no toilet or washing facilities. The marina is in the Westerhaven which is entered through an *ophaalbrug* at the end of the Middenhaven: opening Mon–Fri 7–12, 13–18, 19–20h; Sat, Sun, hols 7.30–12, 13–18, 19–21.30h. The Westerhaven is a rectangular basin, set in very pleasant surroundings of trees and lawns. The marina boxes are on the northern side. A single building houses the Harbourmaster's office, toilets, (coin) showers and launderette. There is a charge for drinking water.

The most lively time to visit Medemblik is during the annual steam festival on the third weekend in June. The streets are full of working steam engines and the harbour with steam tugs, some of which make the journey from England.

There is a fair and frequent miniature steam trains to Hoorn. At any other time Medemblik seems a sleepy little town, with its shops and a very good chandlery just a few minutes from the marina. The town was once a fortified stronghold of the Frisian kings, as evidenced by the 8th century Radboud castle on the S side of the Oosterhaven. Rebuilt in the 13th century, it now houses a collection of coins and antiques. There are some lovely old buildings on the road from the castle to the town centre.

The conspicuous white building, mentioned as a landmark, is the Lely pumping station, one of two which pumped out the Wieringermeer, between Medemblik and Den Oever, in 1930. The land was reclaimed before the Zuiderzee was sealed off and is the only IJsselmeer polder to have been reclaimed from sea water. In 1945 it was flooded again when the retreating Germans blew up the dykes, but this time it was fresh water and within a year it was drained and producing crops.

To the SE of Medemblik the chart shows the village of Andijk and a nearby marina at Kerkbuurt. Andijk was the site of the first experimental Zuiderzee polder, reclaimed in 1926; it was intended as a small-scale scientific study of the problems involved. The experience gained greatly facilitated the subsequent project.

The Afsluitdijk

The dam has locks at each end for passage between the IJsselmeer and the Waddenzee (chart 1810.3). About 3 miles from the W end the 'De Vlieter' monument commemorates its final closure at that point in 1932. It is a popular tourist attraction and there is a very good view from the top. There is a landing place about halfway along the Afsluitdijk at Breezanddijk (chart inset); it is a work harbour and affords an opportunity of going ashore to view the Frisian Islands across the Waddenzee. There are two stages where you can moor and climb to the top of the dam. You will see a similar work harbour on the seaward side.

The lock at Den Oever (chart 1810.6) at the W end of the Afsluitdijk, links the Waddenzee and IJsselmeer. It is about 11 miles from Den Helder. From seaward there is a buoyed channel into the outer harbour which is well sheltered by moles on each side. Proceed down the outer harbour to the Afsluitdijk and moor to the piles while waiting for the two swing bridges to open. Then enter the Voorhaven and proceed to the lock (Stevinsluizen). Once through the lock into the IJsselmeer there are two mooring places: for temporary berths, alongside in the inner harbour *(binnenhaven)*; for overnight stays, in a small marina with all facilities at the S end of the Zuiderhaven (situated at the end of the *binnenhaven* on its W side). Opening times of the bridges and lock are: Mon–Sat 5–21h; Sun, hols 8.30–11, 14.30–17h. Use VHF channel 20 if necessary.

The Kornwerderzand lock (chart 1810.6) at the E end of the Afsluitdijk also links the Waddenzee and IJsselmeer. The nearest port on the seaward side is Harlingen, which is about 8 miles to the N and an access point for the Friesland lakes described in Chapter 12. On the seaward side the Buitenhaven has mooring posts where you can wait in the shelter of the moles for a favourable tide to Harlingen. Two swing bridges lead into the Voorhaven; this, too, has mooring posts and leads through the Lorentzsluizen into the Binnenhaven and the IJsselmeer. A mooring stage on the W side of the

Binnenhaven is a convenient place to get ashore to visit the gun emplacements by the S carriageway; they now form part of a museum commemorating the heroic Dutch defence of the locks in 1940. The locks and bridges open at all times and listen on VHF channel 18.

The remaining ports on chart 1810.3 are all on the E shore of the IJsselmeer and comprise the old Friesland towns of Makkum, Workum, Hindeloopen, Stavoren and Lemmer; and the former island of Urk.

Makkum

The entrance is shown on a larger scale on chart 1810.6. Only 2 miles from the locks at Kornwerderzand, Makkum is a convenient port of call when entering or leaving this side of the IJsselmeer; it provides access to Friesland, but not for yachts drawing over 2 m.

The entrance channel, the Makkumerdiep, has a small marina (Jachthaven W.V. Makkum) on its S bank. At the E end of the Makkumerdiep, on its N side, there is a large stretch of shallow sheltered water which provides a good anchorage. But if you wish to visit the town, the most convenient place to stay is the Visserhaven, which extends S from the seaward end of the lock. It is occupied by the fishing fleet, but there is a yacht mooring stage beyond the fishing boats. There is toilet and (coin) shower block and a water hose on the fish quay.

If your draft is less than 2 m and you intend to proceed inland to the lake district, enter the lock and tie up to the rope loops along its walls. There is a swing bridge over the lock and a fee is payable for passage inland. Beyond the lock, yachts can moor to the wall on either side of the inner harbour. This is a typical Dutch yacht basin with an *ophaalbrug* (the Vallatsbrug) at its far end and lovely old houses dating back to 1688 on each side. The lock and bridges are manually operated. Beyond the Vallatsbrug, boats can moor along both sides of the Turfmarkt as far as the new *ophaalbrug* at the end of the old town. From there it is possible to go via the Van Panhuyskanaal and Bolsward to Sneek, but that belongs to chapter 12. Opening times of the lock and bridges are: Mon–Sat 8–20h; Sun, hols 8–10, 17–19h.

The pleasant little town is noted for its pottery. It has some fine old buildings, particularly the weighhouse which now houses a pottery museum and the vvv. There is a chandlery, small supermarket and fried fish take-away; and chips are obtainable until 23h.

Workum

Continuing S from Makkum along the Friesland side of the IJsselmeer, the next port is Workum which is an access point to the nearby lake district for craft drawing less than 2 m. The entrance channel Het Zool is a mile long (chart inset). The large marina 'It Soal' with all facilities is on the N bank; and two smaller ones, with box moorings and diesel, are a little farther on, but here the depth is just under 2 m. The entrance channel ends at a lock and expands into a small basin where you can moor alongside the landing stages overnight or while waiting to enter the lock. The basin has a toilet block with (coin) showers and a water hose. It is just a short walk into town from the yacht

Workum: author's catamaran moored in lock basin. Lock gives access to town and Friesland Lakes. It is more convenient to stay in the basin if not proceeding to the lakes.

basin, so there is little point in proceeding through the lock unless bound for the lakes.

If continuing inland there is a bascule bridge over the lock, where a fee is payable, and another three bascule bridges in the town. Opening times of the lock and bridges are: Mon–Sat 8–12, 13–17, 18–20h; Sun, hols 9–12, 14–17, 18–20h. On the inland side of the lock there are mooring stages and the De Hoop shipyard where traditional wooden boats are still built or restored, using traditional hand tools. The first bridge after the lock is the Zuiderbrug and the next is the Bagijnebrug: between them it is possible to moor to the S bank of the Diepe Dolte. The third and last town bridge is the manually operated Noorderbrug. Between the last two the Doltewal, on the N bank of the Diepe Dolte, makes a convenient shopping stop only a few minutes from the marketplace. Just before the Noorderbrug there is a marina with a diesel fuelling stage at its entrance.

The town has some well preserved old buildings and water pumps. The vvv and a museum are found in the 1650 weighhouse. There is a small but adequate shopping centre.

Hindeloopen

Just a mile S of Workum, and on the same chart inset, Hindeloopen offers no access inland but is a deservedly popular yachting centre. The small harbour has mooring space alongside the quays and some box moorings. On the E side of the entrance there is a new marina, Jachthaven Hindeloopen, which is far bigger than the town harbour. It has excellent facilities including a swimming pool, boatyard, sailmaker and launderette. The marina Harbourmaster's office and diesel fuelling are at the entrance; the toilets behind this office are available to users of the town harbour.

The S end of the town harbour has a wooden clock tower and shelter where retired seafarers gather to watch the harbour activity. Adjoining this spot there are the vvv and a quaint manual lock and *ophaalbrug*, but the fixed bridges beyond bar access inland. The old lifeboat house on the W side of the harbour is preserved as a lifeboat museum and is well worth a visit; it contains a model of Hindeloopen harbour in 1930 when it was still a Zuiderzee seaport.

Hindeloopen was once an important and busy port dating back to 1255. Now tourists of many nations come to see its narrow canals and arched wooden bridges, while the quayside cafes and restaurants give it a very lively atmosphere. The 1632 church tower leans slightly and is a conspicuous

Hindeloopen: inland end of lock from harbour. Note the fixed bridge preventing yacht access inland. Harbourmaster's office and vvv at left side of picture.

landmark; the churchyard contains some immaculately kept graves of Commonwealth aircrews. Hindeloopen specializes in ornately carved and painted wooden furniture and this can be seen in many shops and in the Hidde Nijland museum housed in the former town hall. There is no shopping centre as such, but a butcher, baker, fish and chip shop, supermarket and post office can be found within a few minutes of the harbour.

Stavoren

This busy port 4 miles SW of Hindeloopen has two entrances: a N into the Buitenhaven and a S into the Nieuwe Voorhaven. The former leads to the Spoorhaven (reserved for ferries from Enkhuizen) and the Oude Haven, where yachts moor alongside the quay landing stages and traditional Dutch sailing barges make a very picturesque scene. It has a small toilet block but no showers. The Nieuwe Voorhaven contains a lock into the Johan Frisokanaal for all the Friesland lakes and waterways. This route is suitable for yachts drawing 2 m. There are mooring stages on the seaward side of the lock at the S end of the Nieuwe Voorhaven, but if proceeding inland the best place to stop is through the lock.

The lock is called the Johan Frisosluis and has low walls with a handy

Stavoren: Oude Haven as seen from Ijsselmeer end. Dutch sailing barges moor to the left side and visitors to the right. Town centre at top side of picture.

127

mooring rail on top. There is an *ophaalbrug* across the inland end of the lock; opening times are Mon–Fri 7–21h; Sat 7–20h; Sun, hols 9–12, 14–17, 18–20h. There are mooring stages on both banks at the inland side for boats awaiting opening.

After passing through the lock from seaward there is an inlet on the N side of the canal where yachts can moor alongside, around a small island at its entrance. There is a bridge from the island to the Schans, which is the W side of the inlet with alongside mooring space for yachts as far as the Koebrug. There is a toilet and (coin) shower block, with a water hose, immediately S of this bridge; and a fuelling stage S of the shower block.

The town is much smaller than seems warranted by the size of the port. Its tiny shopping centre contains a supermarket, baker, butcher, post office, vvv, chandleries and take-away snacks. The S side of the lock is dominated by a huge pumping station which is open to the public.

Lemmer

This is the last of the IJsselmeer ports with direct access to the Friesland lakes. If bound there, with a draft more than 2 m, the town can be missed by entering the Prinses Margrietkanaal directly from the IJsselmeer. The canal entrance is 1 mile W of the town harbours and is shown on a larger scale on chart 1810.6. However, the town is well worth a visit and there is a route via the town, through a lock and three bridges, which connects with the Prinses Margrietkanaal if you wish to go on to the lakes (see Chapter 12).

Direct entry to the Prinses Margrietkanaal from the IJsselmeer is through a buoyed channel, and also indicated by a procession of commercial traffic. Half a mile beyond the entrance there is a large lock, the Prinses Margrietsluis, with an *ophaalbrug* over its N end. It listens on VHF channel 20 and opens: Mon 4–24h, Tue–Fri 0–24h, Sat 0–20h. There is no service on Sundays and public holidays, but passage of the canal is possible on those days via the route through the town. There are mooring stages at both ends of the lock and a small craft waiting area on the N side at the E bank. Water hoses are available in the lock. Half a mile N of the lock, on the E bank, the route via Lemmer town enters the Prinses Margrietkanaal via the Stroomkanaal.

The town of Lemmer is approached via the Lemstergeul channel along the N shore of the Noordoostpolder (chart 1810.6). There is a choice of marinas in the town harbours, but a convenient place to stop for a visit is the town centre itself. Proceed from the Lemstergeul into the Buitenhaven, as shown by the arrowed red dotted line on the chart. Make for the town lock called the Lemstersluis, easily recognized by a conspicuous tower on each side of the entrance. There are waiting stages outside the lock and opening times are: Mon–Fri 7–21h; Sat 7–20h; Sun, hols 8.30–12, 14–17.30, 18–20h. A fee for the lock and town bridges is collected by the Harbourmaster in the lock. All the town bridges open on approach, at the same times as the lock.

The inland end of the lock opens into a wide basin called the Binnenhaven. Yachts may moor to the walls on each side, but they are rather high and it is preferable to continue through the bascule Oudesluisbrug into a stretch of canal called 't Dok where yachts moor alongside a low wall on either side. The N side is called Korte Streek and the S Lange Streek; both are lined with shops, restaurants, snack bars, a supermarket and a chandlery. There is a toilet/shower block (signposted *toiletgebouw*) in Korte Streek near the

Lemmer: entrance to Lemstersluis from Ijsselmeer. Yachts moor to landing stages on either side of the entrance whilst awaiting entry.

Oudesluisbrug. The mooring places along 't Dok are usually full of boats, and the surroundings of old gabled houses and pavement cafes provide a memorable amalgam of Continental vitality and charm. The town centre is only a few minutes away and is dominated by the 1716 church belfry. Behind and E of the church are the vvv, post office and telephones; there is a launderette at 76 Lange Streek. Market day is Thursday and late night closing (21h) is on Friday.

If continuing inland to the lake district, pass through the next bridge, the Flevobrug, into the Zijlroede. (Coming from inland towards Lemmer, the fee for passage through the town and Lemstersluis is payable at the Flevobrug.) There are mooring places on both banks of the Zijlroede. Beyond the next bridge is a series of four marinas with diesel on the S bank, and mooring places on the N bank. The Zijlroede then enters the Stroomkanaal, which in turn

129

joins the Prinses Margrietkanaal. At the junction of the Zijlroede and Stroomkanaal, Watersport Centrum Tacozijl on the W bank of the latter has pontoon berths, a supermarket, chandlery and diesel; and undertakes Volvo engine servicing.

Urk

Once an island in the middle of the Zuiderzee, 15 miles offshore, Urk has been brought ashore as part of the Noordoostpolder after a thousand years of isolation retains its importance as the largest fishing port in the Netherlands. It is easily recognizable from seaward, appearing like a village built on a hillside in stark contrast to the otherwise flat landscape. The port is shown as a large-scale inset on chart 1810.5, but there are far more mooring places than the single marina symbol indicates. In fact that symbol denotes the local yacht club, the W.V. Zuiderzee, on the S side of the Werkhaven, whose moorings are usually all occupied. Visiting yachts can moor alongside the N, S and W walls of the Nieuwe Haven, all three walls of the Westhaven and the S wall of the Oosthaven. Fuel is obtainable from the bunker boats at the S wall of the Westhaven. The vvv on the town waterfront has a toilet and (coin) shower block which is open 7–23h; there are more toilets on the S side of the Oosthaven.

With narrow alleys and small wooden houses with dark green gables. Urk is similar to the fishing ports of Volendam and Marken; and many of the older inhabitants still wear traditional costume. There is a small shopping centre, and a street market on Wednesdays. Urk had a reputation of being unfriendly towards tourists and visiting yachts, but this is no longer the case, and it is just as crowded with yachts and tourists as Marken and Volendam.

A small fishing museum on the waterfront provides a history of Urk itself, as fishing has always been its livelihood. Above the waterfront, looking out over the IJsselmeer, there is a fishermen's memorial which cannot fail to convey the dangers and tragedies which beset these people. It has a statue of a woman gazing out to sea, and three walls full of the names, ages and vessels of those lost there.

CHAPTER 11

Randmeren

Charts 1810.4 and 5

The Randmeren or peripheral lakes *(fig. 34)* represent all that remains of the SE part of the Zuiderzee after reclamation of the Noordoost and Flevoland polders. One shore is formed by the Flevoland polder, while the other is the original Zuiderzee coast *(fig. 32)*. There are two entrances to the Randmeren: from the S part of the IJsselmeer through the fixed Hollandse Brug, and from the N through the opening Ketelbrug. They all have a buoyed channel 3 m deep and their direction of buoyage is from the Ketelbrug in the N to the Hollandse Brug in the S. Depths of less than 1.3 m are marked with beacons. The three sets of locks along the Randmeren all have the same opening times and use VHF channel 18. They open Mon–Sat 7–12.30, 13–19h; Sun, hols 10–12.30, 13.30–19h.

As the IJsselmeer is so shallow, a nasty short sea can soon be whipped up by winds of force 5 and above. Sailing or motoring to windward in such conditions can at best be wet and uncomfortable, and at worst be nauseous and dangerous. But all that can be avoided by cruising the Randmeren instead. Their narrowness and semicircular course provides good shelter amid pleasant green surroundings, and they are very well endowed with marinas. They must also be very well stocked with fish if the abundance of herons is anything to go by.

Chart 1810.4 *Naarden tot Harderwijk* shows the S entrance to the Randmeren through the Hollandse Brug, a road bridge with a railway bridge alongside. Both are fixed and have a charted clearance of 12.9 m, with clearance gauges on the piers to give the exact figure. Yachts requiring more clearance can only enter the Randmeren through the opening Ketelbrug.

GOOIMEER

The first of the peripheral lakes after passing under the Hollandse Brug is the Gooimeer. The buoyed channel has a depth of 3 m, and 1–2 m outside the buoys. From W to E there are marinas at Naarden and Huizen on the S bank and Almere on the N. There is a small island (De Schelp) with mooring stages close by the entrance channel to Naarden marina.

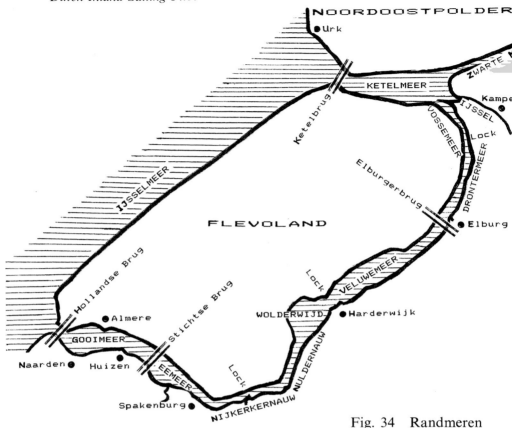

Fig. 34   Randmeren

Almere

Almere is the second of the new towns being built on the Flevoland polder. The first was Lelystad with a projected population of 100,000. Almere is being planned for a population of 250,000, and full use is being made of the experience of building Lelystad and the reactions of its citizens to the environmental features described in the last chapter. The marina (chart inset) has all facilities; it is 10 minutes' walk from a shopping centre and there is a launderette nearby.

Naarden

The first marina on the S side of the Gooimeer is Jachthaven Naarden, close to the old town and entered through a buoyed channel (chart inset). It has box moorings with water hoses and electricity, excellent toilets and showers (coin) and a launderette (tokens) with driers. There are full boatyard facilities, with fuel, chandlery and an engine repair shop which specializes in Yamaha diesels. The fuelling stage has an intercom to call for service when unattended. The marina also has a restaurant, snack bar and a clubhouse with a magnificent central table made from a beautifully varnished leeboard. The town is a half

132

hour walk from the marina but bicycles can be hired from the Harbourmaster. Follow the cycle path under the motorway and head for the square church tower topped with a spire.

Naarden is an old fortified town which was founded in 1350 as a key defensive outpost of Amsterdam. Its most impressive feature is the perfectly preserved star-shaped defensive wall and moat around the town. The best way of seeing Naarden is by following the vvv walking guide. The tower of St Vitus church gives the best view of the fortifications, built to prevent a repetition of the slaughter of the entire population by the Spaniards in 1572. This act is depicted in stone on a 1615 building that now houses a museum devoted to the Czech philosopher Comenius, who is buried here. The present town hall is a fine Renaissance building and the fortress museum in the ramparts is well worth a visit. On some summer Sunday afternoons there are full-costume firings of the cannons, and boat trips round the moat.

Huizen

Once a Zuiderzee fishing village, Huizen has now been so built up and industrialized that little remains of its past. There are two buoyed entrance channels: the W one leading to three marinas; and another at the E end of town which leads through an *ophaalbrug* to a marina by the shopping centre. The bridge opens daily 8.30–22h. Both marinas have toilets and showers.

EEMMEER

Continuing past Almere and Huizen, the 3 m channel moves over to the N bank of the Gooimeer. It then passes under the fixed Stichtse Brug into the Eemeer. This bridge has the same clearance (12.9 m) as the Hollandse Brug. Just past the bridge, off the S side of the channel, is an island called Dode Hond where you can stop overnight free of charge, but the depth is only 1.5 m. Beyond the island a buoyed southbound channel leads into the River Eem. It is shown on the chart inset as Eemmond and has a small marina, 't Raboes, with all facilities.

Spakenburg

The next marinas are at Spakenburg on the S bank. As shown on the chart inset, the entrance channel is between two walls and boats may moor alongside. The channel then divides into a left-hand fork into the Nieuwe Haven (depth 2.5 m) and a right fork into the Oude Haven (depth 2 m). The former has box moorings belonging to the W.V. Eendracht, with toilets, showers and launderette. In the Oude Haven there are box moorings on the N side and alongside berths on the S wall. A landing stage with a water hose is on the N side and a toilet and (coin) shower block. The closed end of the Oude Haven is very picturesque as it is full of traditional Dutch sailing barges in their original Zuiderzee harbour. There is a good shopping centre with plenty of take-aways just a few minutes from the moorings. The town of Spakenburg is continuous with Bunschoten and both places are noted for the traditional costume worn by their women.

Just past Spakenburg, the chart inset shows another marina on the Flevoland shore; the Eemhof marina with all facilities.

Spakenburg: Oude Haven with Dutch sailing barges moored alongside original Zuiderzee harbour. Visiting yachts moor at the entrance to Oude Haven at top of picture.

NIJKERKERNAUW

This is the name given to the very narrow continuation of the Randmeer from Spakenburg to Nulderhoek. It has a lock called the Nijkerkersluis halfway along its length. Just before the lock, on the S bank, is the entrance to Nijkerk marina. This has all facilities and is about half an hour's walk from the town. The lock has mooring stages at each end and an opening bridge across the entrance; it listens on VHF channel 18.

NULDERNAUW and WOLDERWIJD

The Nijkerkernauw ends at Nulderhoek where, on the S bank, Jachthaven Nulde has all facilities. The lake then turns sharply N and changes its name to Nuldernauw. This continues for 3 miles, and then expands into a much wider stretch of water called the Wolderwijd.

A large marina at the entrance to the Wolderwijd and on the Flevoland shore is entered through a buoyed channel. It has all facilities including launderette, fuel, sail loft, engine repairs and boatyard. If you do not require marina facilities, there are overnight mooring places on the island of De Zegge, between the marina and the main buoyed channel, and on the island of De Biezen at the N end of the lake; but both have depths of less than 2 m.

Harderwijk

The channel then passes through the middle of the Wolderwijd until it reaches the Knardijk dam which is the boundary between South and East Flevoland. Here there is a choice of turning SE to the town of Harderwijk or continuing through the Hardersluis lock into the next lake, the Veluwemeer. The lock has two opening bridges.

The channel to Harderwijk is shown on the chart inset. A buoyed eastward branch leads to 'De Knar' marina. There is another nearer town called Jachthaven Zegers BV: to reach it continue along the main channel to Harderwijk and take the first inlet to starboard, just past the Dolphinarium. Both marinas have box moorings and all facilities.

Harderwijk is an old Zuiderzee trading port and former university town. Among its oldest buildings are the 13th century Protestant church and a 14th century town gate. One of its most modern buildings is the Dolphinarium, which is reputed to be the best in Europe.

Chart 1810.5 *Harderwijk tot Urk en Genemuiden* covers the remaining peripheral lakes and their N entrance from the IJsselmeer through the Ketelbrug. This opening bridge affords the only entrance to the Randmeren for yachts with a mast height of 13 m. The chart also shows the passage along the River IJssel to Kampen, and the Zwarte Meer which leads to Blokzijl and Giethoorn.

VELUWEMEER

The next lake is the Veluwemeer, which extends from Harderwijk to Elburg and is entered through the Hardersluis lock. Just past the lock there is an overhead cable with a clearance of 28 m. Next come two small islands S of the buoyed channel, but they are closed to visitors during the nesting season (March–June inclusive). On the Flevoland shore just past these islands the Jachthaven Flevostrand is entered through a buoyed channel and is well sheltered. Four more islands are on the S side of the channel where depths are less than 2 m. The first, Pierland, and the third, De Ral, have mooring places where you can stay overnight; but a charge is made as the facilities are provided by the Bremerbergsehoek marina, which is on the Flevoland shore opposite the last island, De Kwak. From here the channel runs close to the Flevoland shore and the lake is much narrower. There is another marina on this side, called 'De Klink'. At the end of the lake there is an opening bridge (Elburgerbrug) which leads to the Drontermeer.

DRONTERMEER

Immediately past the Elburgerbrug, the canal to Elburg runs SE while the main channel continues very close to the Flevoland shore. There are several berthing places along the W shore of the Drontermeer, and one on the island of Eek, but all have less than 2 m. No landing is allowed on the next two islands, Abbert and Reve. The end of the lake is shown on the chart inset as Roggebotsluis. It has a marina on the mainland side with showers, launderette and fuel. The depth here is over 2 m. Beyond this an opening bridge and lock (Roggebotsluis) lead into the next lake, the Vossemeer.

Elburg

This is a gem of a town and a visit is thoroughly recommended. There are berths alongside the S bank of the canal and a limited number inside the town harbour. The harbourmaster's office has a toilet and (coin) shower for visitors. The town is a well preserved Zuiderzee fishing port which retains a medieval atmosphere within its intact and impressive ramparts. The top of the gateway into the town has a beacon which was formerly the harbour lighthouse. The rectangular pattern of cobbled streets contains a very good selection of shops.

VOSSEMEER

The Vossemeer channel runs alongside the Flevoland shore for 4 miles until it enters the Ketelmeer, which completes the chain of peripheral lakes. The Vossemeer has no mooring places and its only island, De Zwaan, is closed to visitors.

Kampen

The River IJssel, a branch of the Rhine, flows into the Ketelmeer where the Vossemeer joins the Ketelmeer. The river is entered through the Keteldiep channel, between two dykes which project into the Ketelmeer. Kampen is an ancient Hansa city and Zuiderzee trading port about 6 miles upriver from the Ketelmeer. The channel has a depth of 3.2 m and is well marked. There is a choice of four marinas in Kampen, all with showers, but probably the most convenient is the one in the Buitenhaven: it is nearest to the town centre and has a diesel pump at the entrance.

Kampen was an important and busy port in the Middle Ages, specialising in the Baltic trade. Thereafter it gradually went into decline as the IJssel silted up and Amsterdam took over. The town reflects its history in many picturesque mediaeval gateways and buildings, but gives a general impression of dilapidation. However, it is a good shopping centre and has all yachting facilities: chandlery, sailmaker, engine repairer and boatbuilder.

KETELMEER

The Ketelmeer is the last of the Randmeren. Continuous with the Vossemeer at its SE end, it extends 6 miles W through an opening bridge into the IJsselmeer. Just past the walled channel to the River IJssel there is a marina on the Flevoland shore (chart inset), entered by way of a buoyed channel. It is the 'Ketelmeer' marina and has all the usual facilities. A marine archaeology museum next to it has an excellent display of Zuiderzee wrecks and their contents. These were revealed when the polders were drained and range from Roman times to the 17th century.

On the opposite side of the Ketelmeer, and shown on a separate inset, there is a *vluchthaven* (see page 52) at Schokkerhaven *(fig. 35)*. This is at the entrance to the Ramsdiep channel which leads to the Zwarte Meer. It has mooring stages but no facilities. However, it is a convenient place for an overnight stay or a visit to the IJsselmeer Polders Museum. This is about half an hour's walk and shows the history of the area, with many ancient finds from

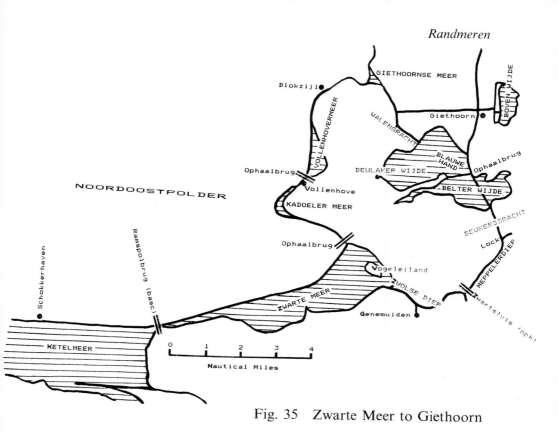

Fig. 35   Zwarte Meer to Giethoorn

its drained sea bed including mammoth bones.

The Ketelbrug over the IJsselmeer end of the Ketelmeer clears less than 13 m; but there is an opening section for taller craft and clearance gauges on the piers. It opens daily at 8.30–12, 13.30–16, 18.30–20. 30h and uses VHF channel 18. Yachts requiring this bridge to open cannot navigate the full extent of the Randmeren as the two fixed bridges at their S entrance (Hollandse Brug and Stichtse Brug) have less than 13 m clearance.

ZWARTE MEER

Sheet 1810.5 and its inset show an E extension of the Ketelmeer. This is the Zwarte Meer, and although not one of the peripheral lakes it is conveniently considered here as it offers a round trip to Giethoorn and Blokzijl (*fig. 35*). Both places are slotted into this chapter as they are too far S to be included in the next one on Friesland. Chart 1810 only shows the Zwarte Meer; but ANWB chart *C: Noordwest-Overijssel* covers the entire round trip.

Schokkerhaven on the N bank of the Ketelhaven is the starting point for this passage. As mentioned earlier, it is a *vluchthaven* with overnight moorings.

The Ramsdiep channel leads E from here into the Zwarte Meer. It is dredged to 3.3 m and has a wall along its S side which extends for 4 miles and separates the navigable channel from the very shallow water of the E Ketelmeer and Zwarte Meer. The Ramsdiep has kilometre posts along the shore of the Noordoostpolder. The first one after Schokkerhaven is km 39, and there is an 83 m tower at km 42. At km 44 there is an opening bridge with mooring stages on both sides. This is the Ramspol bascule bridge which opens: Mon–Fri 6.30–22h; Sat 6.30–18.30h; Sun, hols 9.30–12.30, 14.30–17h.

Just past km 45 on the E side of the bridge, the S wall of the Ramsdiep ends and the S extent of the channel is marked by starboard-hand buoys instead. Km 47 is the entrance to the Zwarte Meer, but the Ramsdiep continues along the shore of the Noordoostpolder as far as km 52, with starboard-hand buoys throughout its length. Outside the channel the depth is barely 1 m. Beyond km 52 the channel leaves the shore and is marked by port and starboard hand buoys as it passes through the centre of the Zwarte Meer. The E end of the Zwarte Meer is blocked by a nature reserve island called Vogeleiland. Landing is prohibited and the Ramsdiep channel ends here as a T-junction, with a northbound arm called the Zwanendiep and a southbound arm called the Zwolse Diep. These two channels are well buoyed and there are leading lights into them as the buoys are unlit.

ANWB Chart C *Noordwest Overijssel* takes over at Vogeleiland from chart 1810. The Zwanendiep leads N from the Zwarte Meer to Vollenhove and Blokzijl, while the Zwolse Diep leads S to Meppel and Zwolle. The round trip described below does not go to the latter two places but follows a circular route via the Zwolse Diep, Meppelerdiep and Beukersgracht to Giethoorn; returning to the Zwarte Meer through the Blauwe Hand and Giethoornse Meer lakes to Blokzijl, Vollenhove and the Zwanendiep (fig. 35).

The channel SE from Vogeleiland along the Zwolse Diep has extensive reed beds on each side, and it is still essential to keep within the buoyed channel as there is only $\frac{1}{2}$ metre depth outside. At km 20 there is a small *vluchthaven* on the S bank of the Zwolse Diep. A little further on at km 19, beware of a cable ferry (*kabel pont*) which crosses over to Genemuiden on the S bank. There are yacht berths and a toilet/shower block in the entrance canal to Genemuiden.

A mile beyond Genemuiden there is a choice of marinas at the town of Zwartsluis. Passage from here into the Meppelerdiep is through an *ophaalbrug* over the open Meppelerdiepkeersluis, on the E side of the waterway. The bridge opens Mon–Sat 6.30–20h; Sun, hols 7.30–8.30, 19–20h. On the N side of the bridge, at the E bank, the W.V. de Kranerweerd marina has all facilities, including fuel and a launderette. On the W bank the Jachthaven Zomerdijk has showers and a Volvo service agency.

Just under 2 miles past Zwartsluis, leave the Meppelerdiep and turn N into the Beukersgracht through the Beukerssluis and *ophaalbrug*. Opening times are Mon–Sat 7–12, 13–20h; Sun, hols 8.30–12, 14–19h. It is an easy lock to negotiate as there are rope loops along the walls. The lock keeper issues an excellent free leaflet containing a map of the local waterways and details of mooring places, marinas, refuse disposal etc. The Beukersgracht ends a mile past the lock where it enters a large lake. This is divided by a dam into a S section called Belter Wijde, a NE section called Blauwe Hand and a NW section called Beulaker Wijde. There is a good mooring place on the W bank where the Beukersgracht enters Belter Wijde. Continue through the Belter

Wijde along the channel; it has a wall on the W side and starboard-hand buoys on its E side. The channel is a mile long and ends at an *ophaalbrug* which opens at the same times as the lock in the Beukersgracht and leads into Blauwe Hand. The buoyed channel divides here, one going N to Giethoorn and the other leading diagonally across the lake towards Blokzijl.

Giethoorn

The channel from the *ophaalbrug* to Giethoorn is called the Kanaal Beukers-Steenwijk and its first mile is separated from Blauwe Hand lake by a wall. A gap halfway along the wall leads to an overnight mooring stage in the lake, alongside a peninsula-like branch of the wall. Half a mile on, the floating Giethoorn vvv office is moored at the E bank of the canal beside the road. Go alongside to obtain information on the local attractions. It is just under a mile from here to the *ophaalbrug* at Giethoorn village centre. There are mooring places along both sides of the canal, N and S of the bridge, but for the purposes of this particular round trip there is no need to go through the bridge.

On the S side of the bridge there is a filling station on the E bank, and another opposite in a marina on the W bank. Mobile food shops stop alongside the E bank, and there is a bakery, butcher, supermarket, post office and take-aways along the road which leads E from the bridge. It runs

Giethoorn: old village showing inaccessibility to cars, with canal bridges as only means of access to houses on the left.

alongside a narrow canal where one can hire punts or outboard dinghies to explore the waterways of the old village of Giethoorn. The end of this canal is the beginning of the old village, which is divided into W and E halves by a waterway. There are no roads here, just a footpath on the W side and arched wooden bridges providing access between thatched houses on each side of the water. Transport throughout this area is confined to bicycles or punts powered by pole or outboard motor, and Giethoorn is known as the 'Dutch Venice'. E of the village canal, channels lead into Boven Wijde, a popular dinghy and board sailing lake.

Giethoorn to Blokzijl

The quickest way is through the Cornelisgracht, just S of Giethoorn bridge, but it is restricted to boats with a beam of less than 2.25 m and draft of 1 m. Larger boats must return S down the Kanaal Beukers-Steenwijk and enter Blauwe Hand lake through the gap in the wall $\frac{1}{2}$ mile S of the vvv. Make for the buoyed channel which leads NW to the Walengracht. If you draft is much more than a metre you will have to continue on S past the gap in the wall and enter the buoyed channel at its entrance, just N of the *ophaalbrug* between Belter Wijde and Blauwe Hand.

At the NW end of the buoyed channel across Blauwe Hand enter the Walengracht, where there are mooring places on the N bank, and further W on the S bank too. At the T-junction with the Vaart Sloot turn N, but beware of a cable ferry at the junction with the Cornelisgracht. There is a mooring place on the E bank just S of the ferry. In the Giethoornse Meer the direction of buoyage changes from that in the Blauwe hand. In the Vaart Sloot and Giethoornse Meer it is from N to S. From the end of the Vaart Sloot head W along the buoyed channel across the S end of the Giethoornse Meer. Then turn SW into the Valse Trog and continue along the Noorderdiep to the *ophaalbrug* and lock at Blokzijl. This leads into the harbour (Havenkolk).

Blokzijl

Opening times of the bridge and lock are: Mon–Sat 8–12, 13–19h; Sun, hols 8.30–12, 14–19h. You may have a long wait for entry at peak holiday times as the lock is quite small. If you arrive at the Noorderdiep end of the lock too late to get through, there are places alongside between the fixed bridges across the inlets on each bank. The N inlet has a vvv mooring stage on the E bank, just S of the fixed bridge. There is a water hose and toilet/shower block through the fixed bridge; showers (coins) are open all night. This inlet runs round Rietvink island and re-enters the Noorderdiep a little farther N, where it is called the Stadsgracht. There are berths all round the island and in the Stadsgracht, though the best place to moor is through the lock in the Havenkolk.

Blokzijl was once a busy port on the Zuiderzee coast, and it seems strange now to see such a large harbour 15 miles inland from the IJsselmeer *(fig. 32)*. However, it is no longer redundant as it has been given a new lease of life by the huge number of pleasure craft which occupy its spacious marina, moored to pontoons and the harbour walls. Toilets, showers and a launderette are housed in the same building as the vvv and open until 22h (launderette tokens from the vvv).

The harbour is surrounded by lovely old houses which display a selection of stepped, bell and neck gables dating back to 1629. A cannon on the quayside formerly sounded the alarm for extra high tides. The narrow cobbled streets radiating from the harbour retain all the charm of their mediaeval past and contain a small but adequate collection of shops.

Blokzijl to Zwarte Meer

The return half of this circular diversion from the Randmeren leaves the Havenkolk through a dangerously narrow floodgate. It stays open, but is only wide enough for one boat and the other side is partially obscured from view, so it is prudent to sound Morse **T** with a foghorn as you approach. Continue for a mile into a small lake called the Vollenhovermeer, where the direction of buoyage is from the Zwarte Meer towards Blokzijl. There is a mooring place at the N end of the lake on the W bank. The Vollenhoverbrug at the S end opens Mon–Sat 7–18h; Sun, hols 10–12.30, 13.30–17h. There are mooring posts on the N side of the bridge; Vollenhove town harbour is on the S side. Visiting yachts are requested to pass through the town *ophaalbrug* into the town harbour where there are moorings with water hoses, toilets and showers; but the depth is less than 2 m. Like Blokzijl, Vollenhove is a former Zuiderzee port *(fig. 32)* which retains many buildings from its prosperous mediaeval past.

A mile from Vollenhove on the W bank there is a small marina just N of the Voorstersluis. The waterway then widens slightly into the Kadoeler Meer for a 2 mile stretch to an *ophaalbrug* over an open lock called the Kadoelerkeersluis. Opening times are: Mon–Fri 7–19h; Sat 7–18h; Sun, hols 10–12.30, 13.30–17h. There is a mooring place at the E bank on the N side of the bridge, should you have to wait. The bridge leads into the buoyed channel of the Zwanendiep at the E end of the Zwarte Meer. From here follow the Ramsdiep back to Schokkerhaven and the Ketelmeer. Thence a choice of returning S into the Randmeren or continuing E through the Ketelbrug into the IJsselmeer.

CHAPTER 12

Friesland

ANWB Chart B: Friese Meren
The coast of the province of Friesland extends between Lemmer, on the IJsselmeer, and Harlingen on the Waddenzee; thence E halfway to the River Ems and Germany. The route to Germany is outlined at the end of this chapter. The main attractions of the province are its IJsselmeer ports *(fig. 36)* and the profusion of lakes occupying the SW region *(fig. 37)*. Access to the lake district is easiest from the IJsselmeer ports of Lemmer, Stavoren and Workum; but they can also be reached from Makkum and the Waddenzee port of Harlingen. However, the routes from Makkum and Workum are only open to yachts drawing less than 2 m. The IJsselmeer ports were covered in Chapter 10 and are only described here insofar as access to the lake district is concerned. Routes to the lakes are shown on ANWB chart B *Friese Meren*, which translates to Frisian Lakes or broads. This chart also shows the IJsselmeer ports, but they are better displayed in chart book 1810.

A brief study of ANWB chart B will show the wide choice of different routes to and between the huge variety of lakes, waterways and villages which constitute this superb cruising ground. It would be too long a task to cover every possibility, so this chapter concentrates on the most direct routes; readers can work out their own variations. It is also difficult to decide where and in what direction to start such an outline. Most yachts would probably be entering via the IJsselmeer ports, but some may come through the province from the N after cruising the Frisian Islands. The chapter accordingly starts with a route from the N and then covers those from the IJsselmeer ports, using the town of Sneek as their meeting point.

Apart from the port of Harlingen, the entire cruising ground is non-tidal fresh water. All marinas in such waters have box moorings and most have coin-operated showers. Farmhouses throughout the province show the characteristic Frisian design of enormous roofs and low walls. One aspect of cruising Friesland which is noticeably different from other parts of the country is that most towns charge for passage through their locks and bridges. A supply of coins should accordingly be kept handy for putting into the clog which is lowered by the bridge keeper as you pass through. Charges range from 2 to 5 guilders. Another useful thing to have is a set of bank mooring spikes. Although most sites have proper mooring stages there remain many spots which could be used if you have spikes.

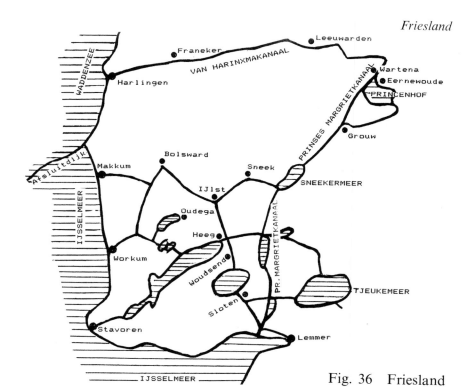

Fig. 36   Friesland

Harlingen

This is the only Friesland port with direct access to the sea. It may be reached from seaward by the routes shown on chart 1811.1, the passage planning sheet of chart book 1811 for the W part of the Waddenzee. This booklet is essential for cruising the Frisian Islands. If you do not have time to visit them, a direct route to Harlingen is the seaward passage from Den Helder (charts 1811.3–5). Follow the buoyed channel from Den Helder to Den Oever, but instead of locking into the IJsselmeer proceed NE along the seaward side of the Afsluitdijk, past the work harbour of Breezanddijk to Kornwerderzand. Again, do not lock into the IJsselmeer but follow the well-buoyed channel N to Harlingen. If coming from the IJsselmeer, pass through the Kornwerderzand lock into the Waddenzee and again follow the channel N to Harlingen. Alternatively, Harlingen can be reached from inland via the Van Harinxma Canal, as described later.

Harlingen is a busy ferry and fishing port so beware of traffic leaving harbour. If in doubt call up Harbour Control on VHF channel 11. The harbour is shown on chart 1811.5 insets, on ANWB chart B and in the Almanak. The best place to moor is in the Noorderhaven: it is the most picturesque part of the town with the best facilities, and is only two minutes' walk from the town centre. Pass through a swing bridge called the Keersluisbrug into the Oude Buitenhaven and then through the Prins Hendrik bascule bridge into the Noorderhaven. These bridges open on the whole and half hour during the following periods: Mon–Sat 6–22h; Sun, hols 7.30–8, 9.30–10, 11.30–12,

(left) Payment for passage through bridge (Bruggeld). Bridge keeper is lowering a clog for collection of coins. The amount is indicated on signposts at bridge approaches.

Harlingen: Noorderhaven showing Jacarah at pontoon berth on north side and alongside berths on south side. Raadhuisbrug and toilet/shower barge off picture to left. Town centre is just beyond the south side of the harbour.

13–13.30; 15.30–16, 17.30–18, 19.30–20, 21.30–22. Boats moor alongside the S wall or to pontoons on the N side that are marked vacant with green labels (red means the owner is returning). They have water hoses and electricity. If the pontoons are all occupied and you have to use the S wall, remember that the water is tidal. There are more pontoon berths on both sides beyond the Raadhuis swing bridge, but this has to be arranged with the Harbourmaster beforehand.

At the end of the Noorderhaven a cream painted barge houses a new toilet and (coin) shower block. Diesel fuel is from a pump on the S side of the Noorderhaven between the Raadhuisbrug and Prins Hendrikbrug. There is a chandlery (Nautic Ring) on the N side and another (Leeuwenbrug B.V.) at the E end of the harbour. The HM can be contacted at the latter chandlery. The Customs office is at the Zuiderhaven, but they usually board visiting yachts in the Noorderhaven.

The Noorderhaven is the oldest part of Harlingen and the yacht basin has a lovely frontage of old houses, with over a hundred gables from the 17th and 18th centuries, many floodlit at night. Other notable buildings are the town hall, and former warehouses named after their trading links, e.g. Java, Sumatra, Polen (Poland) and Ruslan (Russia). The bridge at the E end of the Noorderhaven is called the lions' bridge (Leeuwenbrug) as it is guarded by four ferocious statues. The shopping precinct is only 2 minutes from the harbour and has an adequate collection of shops. The vvv in the precinct issues a free town plan with recommended walks.

If intending to go inland to Leeuwarden along the van Harinxma Canal, an alternative yacht harbour can be found at its entrance. Immediately after entering the canal through the Tsjerk Hiddessluizen, the marina is situated in the inlet to starboard. It has adequate facilities and is only a few minutes from the Noorderhaven.

Van Harinxmakanaal

The canal goes from Harlingen to Leeuwarden, where it joins the route to the River Ems at Delfzijl. But as far as cruising Friesland is concerned, the Van Harinxmakanaal also joins the Prinses Margriet Canal and enables yachts with fixed masts to explore the lake district to the S after first visiting Leeuwarden, the provincial capital *(fig. 36)*.

The canal has only one set of locks, at the seaward end at Harlingen, and there are kilometre posts along the N bank. The locks are called the Tsjerk Hiddessluizen. After leaving the Noorderhaven through the Keersluis swing bridge, turn NE into the Nieuwe Voorhaven and wait for the lock bascule bridge to open. Hours are: Mon–Fri 5–21h; Sat 5–20h; Sun, hols 9–10, 14–15, 18–19h.

The next bridge, a mile farther on, is the bascule Koningsbrug, open: Mon–Fri 7–21h; Sat 7–20h; Sun, hols closed. From here the scenery is pleasant and rural and the canal virtually straight, with little traffic. Frisian cattle graze on either side and birdwatchers will enjoy seeing large numbers of great crested grebes, oystercatchers, coot and herons.

There is another bridge just over 2 miles away at Kiesterzijl, by km 6. This swing bridge opens at the same times as the Koningsbrug. The next one is nearly 2 miles on at the small town of Franeker, but it is well worth stopping to visit the town before passing through this bridge.

Franeker

There is a small marina on the N bank of the canal at km 8, but it has no toilet or shower facilities and is 15 minutes from town. A much better place to stop for a visit is alongside the Zuiderkade by km 9. This is a quiet sheltered inlet on the N side of the canal, a few minute's walk from the town centre and shops.

Franeker is a small town enclosed by a circular canal around the centre and a wall and moat beyond. The main attraction is the planetarium built in 1751 by a self-educated wood worker named Eisa Eisinga. It is the oldest one in the world and a visit is strongly recommended, especially if you are interested in astro-navigation. There is an introductory talk in English followed by a tour of the building. The working representation of the solar system is displayed on the ceiling and the clockwork mechanism which still operates it can be seen in the roof space. Opposite the planetarium is the superb 1591 town hall; the other lovely old buildings are best seen by following the vvv walking guide. Do not miss the old pottery in the 1668 Korendragershuisje.

Franeker to Leeuwarden

Leeuwarden, the capital of Friesland, is 9 miles from Franeker. Leave the latter through the Stationsbrug, open: Mon–Fri 5–21h; Sat 5–20h; Sun, hols 8.30–9.30, 19–20h. Tie up alongside the end of the Zuiderkade on the W side of the bridge whilst waiting. There is a diesel pump and water hose here.

Franeker: town centre with town hall and Belfry. Planetarium is situated off picture to the right, opposite the Town Hall.

Continue along the Van Harinxmakanaal for 3 miles to another bascule bridge by km 16 at Dronrijp; it opens at the same hours as the swing bridge at Kiesterzijl. The next bridge is nearly 3 miles away by km 22 at Deinum, again opening at the same times. There is a mooring inlet on the S bank at its W side. On the E side it is possible to moor alongside the bank.

The next bridge is by km 23 at Ritzumazijl, again a bascule bridge open at the same times. After passing through, leave the Van Harinxmakanaal by taking the NE fork, sign-posted Dokkum, into the Bisschopsrak. Continue E through an open railway swing bridge to the Hermesbrug on the edge of Leeuwarden.

Leeuwarden

The Hermesbrug is a bascule bridge which leads into the Harlingervaart, shown on the plan of Leeuwarden in the Almanak. All the bridges through the city open: Mon–Fri 6–7.15, 8.30–12.15, 13.30–16, 17.30–20.30h; Sat 7.30–12.15, 13.30–18.30h; Sun, hols 9–11, 18–20h.

At the next, the Vallatsbrug bascule, the keeper will lower a clog for the fee for passage through the bridges. This bridge leads N into the Singel, ringing the old city. This section of the canal is called the Westersingel and boats can moor on either side within view of the leaning tower of Leeuwarden. The E side is best as it has a grassy bank, whereas the W side is a wall alongside a noisy, busy road. However, the best place to moor is through the next bridge, the Vrouwenpoortsbrug bascule that leads into the pleasant surroundings of the Prinsentuin park. There are mooring posts here along the grass slopes of the E bank, in a lovely setting surrounded by trees and only 10 minutes from the city centre. There is a water hose on the bank by a space reserved for boats replenishing their tanks. Just through the trees, opposite the bandstand, is a toilet block with showers. The park also contains the provincial library and archives; and a monument to members of the Dutch Resistance, thousands of whom suffered the same fate at the hands of the Germans as their ancestors did from the Spaniards.

To explore the city centre, go to the vvv at the station where you are given a free walking plan and list of attractions in English. Perhaps the most interesting buildings are the leaning tower of Leeuwarden and Mata Hari's house, both within 5 minutes of the yacht moorings. The former is the square Oldenhove tower and the most conspicuous landmark in the city. Mata Hari's house was the home of the World War I spy. Other notable buildings are the 1598 weighhouse and St Boniface church. There is a good selection of museums: natural history, literature, art and Frisian history from the earliest settlers through World War II. The latter story is told in the Resistance (*Verzets*) museum. The vvv leaflet includes the museums.

There is an extensive shopping centre along the banks of a canal, with many narrow lanes leading off that are full of shops and too narrow for cars. Market days are Monday, Friday and Saturday.

If you intend proceeding via Dokkum to Delfzijl instead of visiting the lakes, continue from the Prinsentuin park through the next bridge (Noorderbrug) into the Dokkumer Ee *(fig. 38)* as shown in the Almanak.

Leeuwarden approaching Vrouwenpoortsbrug from Prinsentuin Park on return passage from Leeuwarden to van Harinx Makanaal. Leaning Tower in background.

Leeuwarden to the Lakes

The Friesland lakes are grouped mainly in the SW corner of the province, and though they are most conveniently entered from the IJsselmeer ports, all can be reached from Leeuwarden and the route from there will be described first. Just S of Leeuwarden there is a vast nature reserve called the Princenhof which should not be missed on your way to the other lakes. It has a large-scale inset on ANWB chart B and consists of lakes and extensive reed beds intersected by a variety of narrow channels, but depths are less than 2 m.

Leeuwarden is left by the way you came in, so return from the Prinsentuin park through the Vrouwenpoortsbrug, Vallatsbrug, Hermesbrug and the open railway bridge (there is no charge for the outward passage). Immediately after the open railway bridge, ignore the waterway leading S and take the next exit from the Bisschopsrak back to the Van Harinxmakanaal between km 23 and 24. Just S of km 24 is a railway swing bridge, open Mon–Fri 6–21h; Sat 6–20h; Sun, hols closed. Exact times are in the ANWB leaflet.

A mile on is another railway swing bridge alongside a road bascule bridge; they open at the same times as the previous one. Next come two bascule bridges, side by side, at km 27, which also open at the same times. There is a mooring stage on their E side. The last of the Leeuwarden bridges is the bascule Drachtsterbrug between km 28 and 29 which opens at the same times as the previous ones.

Continuing E from the Drachtsterbrug, there is an intersection with another waterway at km 30. An island here extends as far as Altenburg, with a convenient mooring stage at km 31, just S of the windmill. The island is rather like the Haringvreter island in the Veerse Meer, with paths through the woods, an abundance of rabbits, and picnic sites and refuse bins. There is a small marina on the N side. The route to the Princenhof continues S from Altenburg for 1 mile to km 33 where it turns E into the Lange Meer and Schalke Diep. Between km 36 and 37, near buoy no. 1, there is a mooring place by the roadside on the S bank. Just beyond, the Van Harinxmakanaal ends at its junction with the Prinses Margriet canal at Fonejacht. At this point take the hairpin bend S into the Prinses Margriet canal where there is a bascule bridge, the Fonejachtbrug, that opens: Mon–Fri 8–21h; Sat 8–20h; Sun, hols 9–12, 14–17, 18–20h. There is a fuelling barge at the W bank on the S side of the bridge. Just over a mile from the bridge, past km 51, is the N end of the Princenhof, but before entering this delightful area a short diversion to Wartena makes a pleasant stop. If your draft is over 2 m, continue along the Prinses Margrietkanaal to Grouw *(fig. 36)*, ignoring Wartena and the Princenhof.

Wartena

The route into Wartena from the Prinses Margrietkanaal is clearly shown on the chart inset. Turn N into the Rogsloot and proceed to the provincial *ophaalbrug*, open: Mon–Sat 9–12, 13–17, 18–20; Sun, hols 9–12, 14–17, 18–20h. A marina on the S side of the bridge at the E bank has box moorings and a fuelling stage. Turn W after the bridge, past a small marina on the S bank, to the village *ophaalbrug*. This opens at the same times as the other but a fee is charged. There is a sheltered mooring space through the bridge alongside the banks. The little village has a supermarket, snack bar and a boatyard.

To explore the Princenhof it is necessary to return the same way from Wartena, again paying at the village *ophaalbrug*. Continue across the Prinses Margrietkanaal into the Princenhof along the Lange Sloot. If you wish to stop for shopping or a restaurant meal, the only place in the Princenhof is the village of Eernewoude at the end of the Lange Sloot.

Eernewoude

Follow the port-hand buoys along the Lange Sloot and Siegersdiep past the Hotel Princenhof on the N bank; it has moorings for customers and a fuelling stage. From the hotel turn NE into a small lake called the Eernewoudster Wijd, where the village yacht basin will be found on the port side of the entrance. It has box moorings, a filling station and a toilet block with (coin) showers. If this harbour is full there is another near the end of the lake on the W bank, with the same facilities. The village is uninspiring but has a small supermarket, a butcher and a restaurant.

Princenhof

This area of rural lakeland is a maze of small lakes, reed-fringed islands and interconnecting narrow waterways which are 1–2 m deep. In some parts it resembles lake scenes from the classic film 'African Queen'. Some of the channels between the reed beds are so narrow that an extra lookout for oncoming boats is necessary, especially if you are aboard a catamaran. Passing places may be few and far between in the narrowest channels and it may be necessary to pull in to the side to allow oncoming traffic to get past. In doing so, beware of entangling your crosstrees or masthead in the real trees. One such channel with a very picturesque windmill on the bank is the Nauwe Saiter, running SW from the Lange Sloot.

However, do not let this account deter you. The whole area is an absolute delight for those who wish to get away from an urban environment and explore unspoilt natural surroundings. The inset on ANWB chart B will show how much scope there is for taking a variety of routes around and between the islands. There are innumerable mooring places throughout the area where you may stop for a meal or overnight in perfect solitude. Alternatively you can anchor in shallow, sheltered water with nothing but the sounds of wildlife and the gentle lapping of water. Birdwatchers will have a feast of sightings, including black terns which are quite common hereabouts.

Princenhof to Grouw and the Lakes

The quickest ways to Grouw from the Princenhof are via the Prinses Margrietkanaal, having returned N towards Wartena, or W from Eernewoude along the Folkertssloot. But the pleasantest route is S from the Princenhof into a mile long lake called the Sijtebuurster Ee. This may be entered from the SW corner of the Princenhof via the Geeuw and Graft. Alternatively proceed S from Eernewoude along the Hooidamsloot to the *ophaalbrug* at its S end, open Mon–Fri 7–21h; Sat 7–20h; Sun, hols 9–12, 14–17, 18–20h. There is a marina with toilet/shower facilities on the S side of the bridge. From here proceed W through the Kromme Ee, with mooring places all along the N bank.

The spacious sailing area of the Sijtebuurster Ee allows an enjoyable change from the motoring which is unavoidable in narrow waterways. There are plenty of mooring places on all sides among quiet rural surroundings. The W end of the Sijtebuurster Ee is continuous with the Pik Meer which runs N to the yachting centre of Grouw.

Before proceeding to Grouw, those who like squeezing broad-beamed boats through narrow spaces may traverse the Goengahuister Sloot on the S side of the Sijtebuurster Ee. This begins and ends with an open lock which is only 5 m wide and is particularly hair-raising for catamaran helmsmen. However, there is a just reward at the W end where, after safely emerging through the lock gates, there is a delightful mooring place on the N bank opposite a windmill. Here the helmsman may well be in need of a cup of tea or something stronger.

Grouw

The small town of Grouw is situated at the confluence of five waterways and accordingly offers a good selection of marina berths, filling stations and boatyard facilities. From S to N, the Pik Meer bank has a series of box moorings with a toilet/shower block close by the 'Theehuis' and the 'Engelse Pub', and less than 10 minutes from the shops. There are also some convenient berths for this purpose at the junction of the Pik Meer and Rechte Grouw, alongside the Nieuwe Kade and the Suderkade, less than 5 minutes from the shops.

The Nieuwe Kade has an alongside mooring space opposite the Restaurant Pierrot where the tourist boats moor, but it is vacant and available to visiting yachts 17–09h. The Nieuwe Kade has a sailmaker, chandlery, and repair workshop specializing in Volvo engines. Continuing from Nieuwe Kade past the white Oostergoo Hotel and the youth hostel, there are alongside berths and a water hose at the Suderkade. An excellent little shopping centre close by the Nieuwe Kade and Suderkade caters for all tastes, including fish and chips, and has toilet/shower facilities in what looks like a private house. Although undistinguished architecturally, Grouw has a special yachting atmosphere akin to that of Burnham-on-Crouch.

Grouw to Sneekermeer

The Sneekermeer is a large lake that offers some interesting cruising and is a deservedly popular yachting centre. The most direct route from Grouw is along a 4 mile stretch of the Prinses Margrietkanaal: it passes right through the Pik Meer and runs along the E side of Grouw. This is the only way for yachts drawing over 2 m. A mile from the Pik Meer at km 61 there are two bascule bridges, side by side; they listen on VHF channel 18 and open: Mon 4–24h; Tues–Fri 0–24h; Sat 0–20h; Sun, hols 9–12, 14–17, 18–20h.

The last bridge before the Sneekermeer is another mile on by km 63. There are mooring places on both sides of the canal just before it, where another waterway cuts across. This is the Oude Schouw bascule bridge, open: Mon–Fri 8–21h; Sat 8–20h; Sun, hols 9–12, 14–17, 18–20h. Two miles on the canal enters the Sneekermeer through a pair of locks at Terhorne: they remain open and there is one-way traffic through each. The canal side of the locks has marinas with diesel pumps on the N and S banks.

A longer but more interesting route from Grouw to the Sneekermeer goes via the Pik Meer and Akkrum. Proceed SE from Grouw through the Pik Meer, taking care not to enter the Prinses Margrietkanaal by mistake. Continue to the end of the lake and head S into the Graft: there are mooring places just here at the E bank. Proceed via the tiny Bokkumermeer to the Nesserzijl *ophaalbrug* on the outskirts of Akkrum, the first of five bridges at Akkrum which all open at the same times: Mon–Sat 9–12, 13–17, 18–20h; Sun, hols 9–12, 14–17, 18–20h. On the W side of this bridge at the S bank there is a marina with diesel. The third is a railway swing bridge with moorings on its W side. The fourth is the municipal *ophaalbrug* where a fee must be placed in the clog lowered by the keeper. The fifth and last bridge is another *ophaalbrug* which leads into the Meinesloot where, on the S bank, there is mooring space between two marinas. The westernmost marina, Tusken de Marren, is the largest and best appointed.

The very small town centre of Akkrum is 10 minutes from the marina. It has a supermarket, butcher, baker, post office, bank and vvv office. Unless you need to go shopping, there is nothing else to recommend a visit. It is just over a mile from the Meinesloot bridge to the Sneekermeer, but there are some good mooring places before that, at the junction of the Meinesloot and Henhuisterdeel.

Sneekermeer

This superb expanse of water has ample room for sailing and a buoyed channel for traffic using the Prinses Margrietkanaal. Outside the buoyed channel depths are under 2 m. It is one of the most popular dinghy racing centres in the country, but its islands and variety of channels make it a favourite cruising area too, with an abundance of birdlife such as great crested grebes, common and black terns, herons, coot and mallard. Like the Princenhof there are ample mooring facilities: landing stages throughout the lake sides and on the islands, together with a selection of marinas for those who want the facilities they provide. The lake is accessible via the Princes Margrietkanaal, from Grouw to the N and Lemmer to the S; and from Stavoren, Workum or Makkum to the W.

As mentioned earlier, the Prinses Margrietkanaal leaves for Grouw from the N of the lake through an open pair of locks called the Terhornesluizen. There are marinas with fuel immediately E of the locks on each bank. The large island of Terhorne S of the locks is accessible by road via an *ophaalbrug* at each end of the island. There is a small charge each time you pass through either bridge. The N bridge across the Nieuwe Zandsloot opens: Mon–Fri 7–21h; Sat 7–20h; Sun, hols 9–12, 14–17, 18–20h. There are mooring stages on each side. The S bridge across the Heerenzijl opens: Mon–Sat 9–12, 13–17, 18–20h; Sun, hols 9–12, 14–17, 18–20h.

Heading S from the N bridge, the Zandsloot inlet at the NE end of the island has alongside mooring places as far as the fixed bridge at Terhorne village. This is convenient for shopping in the village. From here it is a pleasant sail S, passing through the other bridge to regain the Sneekermeer and complete a trip round the island. It is a popular camping area and is reminiscent of Kaag island in that respect.

At the W end of the Sneekermeer there is a large marina at the Paviljoen Sneekermeer, the Jachthaven Voetveer with all facilities. There are also mooring places all round Starteiland opposite the marina. Starteiland is, as the name implies, an island with a race control tower; but it also has a restaurant with toilet and shower facilities which are available to visiting yachts. If you wish to stop overnight it is best to avoid mooring along the W side of the island as it is exposed to the noise and wash of traffic using the Prinses Margrietkanaal.

Sneekermeer to Sneek

It is 2 miles from the Sneekermeer to Sneek along the Houkesloot, which leaves the SW corner of the lake at the point where the Prinses Margrietkanaal begins its passage through the lake. The direction of buoyage in the Houkesloot is from E to W. There are mooring places on the N bank and a filling station on the S bank before reaching the outskirts of Sneek. Here, about 1½ miles from the lake, a small canal leads from the N bank to three marinas: this is the Jachthavenkanaal or Burg. De Hoopkanaal. There are flats along the canal with mooring reserved for residents; but a T-junction beyond has places for visiting yachts on the N bank. The W (port) arm of the T-junction leads to the Oudevaart marina, while the E (starboard) arm leads to two marinas called Domp 1 and Domp 2. All are set amid the pleasant surroundings of a large park and have box moorings, diesel pumps and showers. Domp 1 seems to be the best appointed of the three: it has finger berths as well as boxes, all with water hoses and electricity, a fuelling stage and a café. Showers are operated by tokens from a slot machine outside. It is 15 minutes from the marina to the town centre, but only 5 minutes to a supermarket, post office and bank. Alternatively, visit the town by dinghy and enjoy the experience of going straight under all the town bridges without having to wait for them to open.

The through route from the Houkesloot into town and out via the River Geeuw is about a mile long, (shown on the chart and in the Almanak). It involves passing through three bridges, open: Mon–Sat 7–8, 9–12, 13–17, 18–21h; Sun, hols 8–9, 14–17, 18–20h. From the marinas re-enter the Houkesloot by the way you came and head NW into the Zomerrak, which is a continuation of the Houkesloot. At the end of the Zomerrak turn left and go through the bascule Oppenhuizerbrug. There is a toilet/shower block on the S bank, at the E side of this bridge. The second bridge is an *ophaalbrug* called the Van Harinxmabrug, and between the two there is a filling station on the N bank. On the S side of the Van Harinxmabrug there is a supermarket at the W bank. The third bridge, at the entrance to the town harbour and River Geeuw, is the bascule Lemmerbrug. All the way from the Oppenhuizerbrug to the Lemmerbrug there are mooring places alongside the banks.

Sneek

The lovely town of Sneek is accessible from the Sneekermeer via the Houkesloot as just described; and via the River Geeuw from the lakes to the SW and their linking IJsselmeer ports. It provides excellent facilities for visiting yachts as it not only has three good marinas on the Houkesloot, but also plenty of mooring places between the opening bridges on the through route around the S side of the old town centre. This is the route just described and is shown in the Almanak and on the ANWB chart. On this route, between

Sneek: Waterpoort as seen from town centre with yacht moorings beyond. Lemmerbrug opening on left.

the Van Harinxmabrug and Lemmerbrug there is another marina in the Woudvaart. It leads off to the S and is entered through an *ophaalbrug* called the Woudsvaartbrug. The marina is just through the bridge, on the W bank, and has a launderette. Beyond, the Woudvaart is impassable to fixed-mast yachts as it has a fixed bridge.

The town harbour or Kolk is a large basin on the N side of the Lemmerbrug. Its W end is continuous with the River Geeuw which is the shortest route from the IJsselmeer ports. The E end is dominated by the spectacular Waterpoort, a beautiful water gate at the entrance to the old town centre built in 1613 as a fortified bridge over the Geeuw. Yachts can moor for overnight stays all round the harbour, except by the Lemmerbrug where there is a reserved space for boats wishing to use the bridge water hose. A charge is payable at the Lemmerbrug for passing from the harbour through to the Houkesloot and Sneekermeer, but not in the reverse direction.

The town centre and vvv are just a few minutes from the Kolk. The vvv provides a free town plan with details in English of the main attractions. These include the 16th century Martini church with a wooden belfry tower; the 15th century town hall; nautical, antiquities and model train museums. There is a good selection of shops in the town centre; and a very large supermarket on the E edge of the old town, by the Leeuwarderbrug on the walking route from the Houkesloot marinas.

155

Stavoren to the Lakes

The route from the IJsselmeer to the lakes via Stavoren *(fig. 37)* is suitable for yachts drawing 2 m. It starts at the lock at the entrance to the Johan Frisokanaal, as described in Chapter 10 and illustrated in the Almanak. Within half a mile from the lock there is a large marina called Jachtservice (Marina) Stavoren on the S bank, and a little further E on the N bank another called Jachthaven de Roggebroek. Both have all facilities, including a launderette at the former.

A mile E of the marinas, at the village of Warns, an *ophaalbrug* called the Warnserbrug opens: Mon–Fri 7–21h; Sat 7–20h; Sun, hols 9–12, 14–17, 18–20h. At the W side of the bridge on the S bank, Warns has a small harbour with yacht berths. On the E side there is Jachthaven Waterlijn on the S bank; another farther E on the N bank, Jachthaven Het Lengerke, has a chandlery and sailmaker.

From here a buoyed channel enters a series of lakes which extend for 8 miles to Heeg. The first one, the Morra, is a mile long and ends at an *ophaalbrug* at Galamadammen that opens at the same times as the bridge at Warns and has mooring posts on each side. Jachthaven De Kuilart at the N bank on the E side of the bridge has box moorings and all facilities, including a launderette.

Fluessen

Continuing NE, the buoyed channel (3.6 m) leads for 4 miles through Fluessen lake. At its entrance, the channel is called the Nieuwe Vaart where it is narrowed by a nature reserve island which is a nesting ground for common

Stauoren: Johan Frisosluis, inland end leading to Friesland lakes. Note the handy mooring rail on top of the lock wall and the mooring stages inland for awaiting opening.

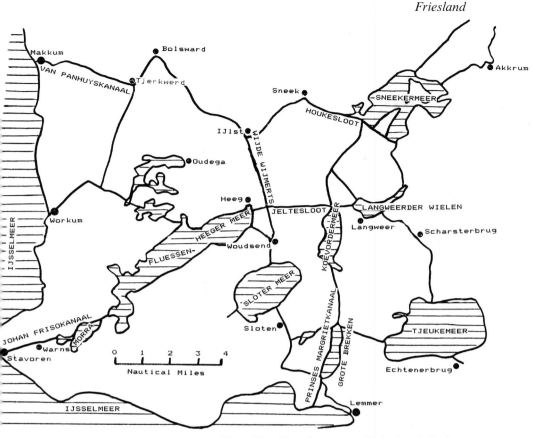

Fig. 37   IJsselmeer to Friesland Lakes

terns and black-headed gulls. There are some mooring places on the S shore of the Fluessen and on a small island called Nije Kruspolle. Its W and N sides have mooring posts, but spikes are necessary on the S side. There is another island mooring place at the N end of the Fluessen. This is the V-shaped island called Langehoekspolle which marks the entrance to a series of small lakes which lead to Workum. These, and the route from Workum, are described later in the chapter.

Heeger Meer

The Fluessen continues into another lake, the Heeger Meer. It has the same depths and carries the buoyed channel of the Johan Frisokanaal. There are two islands with mooring places: Leyepolle, off the S bank at the junction with the Fluessen; and Rakkenpolle at the E end of the Heeger Meer. Just S of the Rakkenpolle a zigzag waterway called the Woudsender Rakken leads to the pleasant little town of Woudsend; wherefrom it is possible to go N to Sneek, E to the Sneekermeer, or S to the Sloter Meer, Sloten and Lemmer. The small town at the end of the Heeger Meer, just N of Rakkenpolle island, is called Heeg.

Heeg: town quay, with sharp turn right foreground through swing bridge. VVV office and toilets are situated across the bridge.

Heeg

Situated near the confluence of a number of waterways which provide cruising routes throughout the whole of Friesland, Heeg is a very popular yachting centre and well endowed with marinas. These are found on both sides of the channel from the Heeger Meer and all have diesel pumps but depths are less than 2 m. There are alongside berths at the town quay S of the swing bridge across the Wegsloot: the VVV and toilets are also there. There is no point in going through this bridge as all subsequent ones are fixed. The town shopping centre is small but adequate and includes chandleries and a sailmaker.

The Johan Frisokanaal regains its canal form at Heeg, continuing E from the Heeger Meer to join the Prinses Margrietkanaal from Lemmer. It affords access to the entire Friesland cruising ground by a variety of routes. These are fascinating to plan from the ANWB chart, but care must be taken to ensure that there are no fixed bridges on the way and that opening times of bridges are suitable. An up-to-date edition of the Almanak is essential for the latter purpose.

Heeg to Sneek

Follow the Johan Frisokanaal buoyed channel from the N end of the Heeger Meer to its junction with the Wijde Wijmerts ½ mile E of Heeg. Turn N into this waterway and proceed for another half mile to the *ophaalbrug* at Osingahuizen. There is a charge at the bridge, which opens: Mon–Sat 9–12, 13–17, 18–20h; Sun, hols 8–9, 14–17, 18–20h. Continue for 2 miles to the small town of IJlst. There are mooring places along the E bank of the Wijde Wijmerts in the last mile before the turn E into IJlst; and more in the town itself. Continue to the *ophaalbrug* over the River Geeuw; it opens at the same times as the previous bridge and a fee is payable. There is an attractive windmill and some mooring places on the E side of the bridge, plus a small marina with showers.

Continue NE along the Geeuw for another mile to a bascule bridge which opens during the same hours as the previous two. It has mooring stages on each side and the last half mile to Sneek has mooring places on the N bank, but continue all the way to the Kolk, which is the name given to the old town harbour of Sneek (already described). From here one may go on via the Lemmerbrug to the Houkesloot for the Sneekermeer and a variety of routes via the Princes Margrietkanaal, e.g. N to Grouw and the Princenhof, or S towards Lemmer.

Lemmer to the Lakes

The route from Lemmer to the lakes goes via the Prinses Margrietkanaal, which is the main route for commercial traffic across Friesland. As explained in Chapter 10, there are two ways of entering this canal: directly from the IJsselmeer a mile W of Lemmer; or through the town bridges into the Stroomkanaal, which joins the Prinses Margrietkanaal a mile or so out of town.

Direct passage into the deep-water Prinses Margrietkanaal and through the Prinses Margrietsluis has already been described. Indirectly from Lemmer, the route to the canal is shown on ANWB chart B; and also on an inset on chart 1810.6 and in the Almanak. Proceed as described in Chapter 10 through the town lock (Lemstersluis) and the Oudesluisbrug to the Flevobrug. Continue through this bridge into the Zijlroede, then through another *ophaalbrug* called the Zijroedebrug, past a series of marinas to a T-junction with the Stroomkanaal. Turn N at the junction and proceed for about ½ mile into the Prinses Margrietkanaal. All the town bridges open at the same times as the Lemstersluis. This is the only way through on Sundays as the lock into the Prinses Margrietkanaal is closed on that day.

Prinses Margrietkanaal

Just N of its junction with the Stroomkanaal, the Prinses Margrietkanaal continues as a buoyed channel (3.6 m) for 2 miles along a narrow lake called the Grote Brekken. There are two mooring places in this lake: the first is at the SW corner where the Langesloot channel branches off to the W; the second is at an island at the N end of the lake. At this end there is a choice of three cruising routes:

1. N along the Prinses Margrietkanaal, via the Koevordermeer, Westerbrug-

sloot and Modderige Geeuw to the Sneekermeer. Thence via the Houkesloot to Sneek; or through the Sneekermeer to Grouw and the Princenhof. This is the only route open to craft with a draft over 2 m.

2. W along the Kromme Ee to Sloten, thence through the Sloter Meer to Woudsend. From there, W to the Heeger Meer, N to Sneek or E to the Koevordermeer.

3. E along the Follega Sloot to the Tjeukemeer.

All three options are considered in order, starting with (1) the continuation of the Prinses Margrietkanaal N from the Grote Brekken. From the latter, head for the conspicuous telecommunications tower at Spannenburg and pass through the bascule bridge, open: Mon–Fri 8–21h; Sat 8–20h; Sun, hols 9–12, 14–17, 18–20h. Just over a mile farther N, past km 82, enter the Koevordermeer and follow the buoyed channel which takes the canal through the lake. Half a mile from its entrance there is a westbound channel called the Welle which has mooring places on its N bank. Although the Welle leads to Woudsend it has a fixed bridge. There are no other mooring places and little of interest in the Koevordermeer, unless you stray a little from the buoyed channel and run aground in the shallow patch to its E. At the N end of the lake there is a choice of continuing along the Prinses Margrietkanaal to the Sneekermeer, or diverting W along the Johan Frisokanaal for Heeg, the Heeger Meer or Woudsend. This diversion will be considered now before resuming the direct route to the Sneekermeer. Yachts drawing 2 m can return this way to Stavoren but are unable to reach Woudsend.

Woudsend

At the N end of the Koevordermeer turn W into the Johan Frisokanaal. This part of it is called the Jeltesloot and is crossed by an *ophaalbrug*, the Jelteslootbrug, just over a mile W of the Koevordermeer. It opens: Mon–Fri 7–21h; Sat 7–20h; Sun, hols 9–12, 14–17, 18–20h. There are mooring stages on both sides of the bridge. Half a mile beyond the bridge there are mooring places on both banks of the canal with two small islands between. Immediately W of these islands there is a choice of three routes: N along the Wijde Wijmerts to IJst and Sneek, as already described in the section on Heeg; W to the Heeger Meer and Heeg, and then back to Stavoren by a route already described, or on to Workum by a route yet to be described; or finally S into the Nauwe Wijmerts for Woudsend and beyond.

The last route is just over a mile long. There is a bankside mooring place at the end of Nauwe Wijmerts, at its junction with the Welle, but it has no access to Woudsend unless you use a dinghy. There are alongside mooring places at the town quay N of the town bridge on the W bank; and just beyond these at the S end of the Woudsender Rakken. There is a large marina on the W side of the Woudsender Rakken, with box moorings, electricity, water taps (no hoses); at the marina entrance is a hose and a toilet block with (coin) showers. There is another marina and boatyard on the S bank of the Welle, 10 minutes' walk from town. It is called 'Koaalite B.V.' and has mooring stages outside the huge hangar-like sheds where large motor cruisers are moored under cover. There are toilets and (coin) showers at the E end of the boatyard buildings.

It is a mile from Woudsend to the Heeger Meer along the zigzag course of the Woudsender Rakken; with a mooring place on the S bank just before it enters the lake. Going S from Woudsend, the River Ee leads to the Sloter

Woudsend: view looking south from town Ophaalbrug towards Sloter Meer. VVV office at end of bridge off left side of picture. Alongside mooring on right side continue north through bridge.

Meer, Sloten and back to Lemmer, as described later.

There is a charge for passage through Woudsend *ophaalbrug*, which opens: Mon–Sat 9–12, 13–17, 18–20h; Sun, hols 9–12, 14–17, 18–20h. There are more mooring places at the W bank on the S side of the bridge. The town is small, neat and tidy with a shopping centre just a few minutes from the boats. It includes a chandlery and take-away chip stalls open until 21h. The VVV is at the E end of the bridge and there is an attractive windmill just S of it on the W bank.

Sloten

The route from Lemmer to the S end of the Grote Brekken has already been described. From here to Sloten there are two routes: via the Langesloot, or from the N end of the Grote Brekken via the Kromme Ee. Neither are accessible to yachts drawing 2 m.

Turn W into the Langesloot immediately after entering the Grote Brekken; there is a mooring place at this corner. Then pass through the Rengersbrug; a charge is payable, and opening is: Mon–Sat 8–12, 13.30–20h; Sun, hols 13–14.30, 18–19.30h. A mile on there is a mooring place at the S bank. The channel then turns N into the Boomsvaart where, 1 mile on, it is joined by the other route from the N end of the Grote Brekken. The latter leaves via the Rijnsloot which has mooring places on the S bank. From here the channel changes names to Kromme Ee, Brande Meer and Woudsloot before entering the Boomsvaart. Sloten is $\frac{1}{2}$ mile N of this junction.

At the end of the Boomsvaart, on the W bank and at the S edge of Sloten, there is a large marina with (coin) showers, and a launderette (tokens from the harbourmaster, post office or vvv). There are some alongside mooring places at the N end of town which are reached by continuing from the Boomsvaart along the E side of Sloten and through the Nieuwe Langebrug. There is a charge for passage through this *ophaalbrug* open: Mon–Sat 9–12, 13–17, 18–20h; Sun, hols 9–12, 14–17, 18–20h. There are toilets and a (coin) water hose for these moorings on the N side of the bridge.

The approach to Sloten from the Boomsvaart reveals a beautiful scene of the old town gate (Lemsterpoort) beside a lovely thatched windmill. The gate crosses a narrow canal through the town centre, where houses date back to the 17th century. Similar buildings are to be found in the narrow cobbled lanes leading off the canal to the star-shaped defensive moat surrounding the town. Sloten received its charter in 1250 and is officially recognised as the smallest town in the Netherlands with a population of only 700. The best way of seeing all its old buildings and remnants of its fortifications is by following the vvv's free town walking guide. The town has just a few shops and is easily accessible as already described, from Sneek in the north and the IJsselmeer ports in the west.

Sloter Meer

North from Sloten along the Slotergat, the Sloter Meer is $\frac{1}{2}$ mile from the town; it is over a mile long and 2 miles wide. The channel (1.8 m) through the lake from Sloten to Woudsend has a direction of buoyage from S to N, but the channel from Balk (at the SW corner of the lake) to Woudsend has an opposite direction of buoyage, from N to S. There are no mooring places or islands in the lake which is a popular dinghy sailing centre. There is a marina at the SW corner in the entrance to the Luts channel which leads to Balk, but access to the town is prevented by a fixed bridge.

The route from Lemmer to Sloten and the Sloter Meer offers further progress N to Woudsend; thence a choice of three routes as already described in the section on Woudsend:
(i) NW to the Heeger Meer and back to Stavoren, or on to Workum;
(ii) N via the Wijde Wijmerts to IJlst and Sneek;
(iii) E via the Johan Frisokanaal and Prinses Margrietkanaal to the Sneekermeer and Sneek.

Tjeukemeer

The route from Lemmer to the Tjeukemeer follows the same path as that to Sloten, but instead of turning W at the N end of the Grote Brekken, turn E into the Follega Sloot. Just over a mile on there is an *ophaalbrug* which opens: Mon–Fri 8–12, 13–20h; Sat 8–12, 13–20h; Sun, hols 8.30–12, 14–17.30, 18–20h. There are stages on both side of the bridge. The buoyed channel at the entrance to the Tjeukemeer is just beyond; with a mooring place on the N bank at the entrance. The whole of the W side of the Tjeukemeer is traversed by a dam carrying a motorway. The only way through this dam is beneath a fixed bridge with a charted clearance of 11.8 m, though the Almanak gives a figure of 12.4 m. Unfortunately there are no clearance gauges on the bridge so you may have an awkward decision to make. A whip VHF aerial makes a

Sloten: view through town centre, looking north from Lemsterpoort towards Sloter Meer.

useful gauge on such occasions if you have the nerve to try it.

If you decide against attempting the bridge, there is an alternative route into the lake from its N end, as described shortly, but this too is closed to yachts drawing over 2 m. The lake is roughly rectangular, 3 miles wide and 2 miles long, but does not offer such a large sailing area as its size suggests as there are several shallow buoyed patches. A buoyed channel to the S side leads to Echternerbrug where there are mooring places and a small marina, but there is little point in continuing through the village as there are fixed ones beyond.

Another buoyed channel leads along the W side of the Tjeukemeer to its N entrance. This one is accessible to yachts unable to pass beneath the fixed bridge in the dam. There is a small island halfway along the dam, with mooring stages on its N and W sides; and another mooring place on a tiny island at the N entrance.

Tjeukemeer to Sneekermeer

Follow the buoyed channel to the N exit from the Tjeukemeer and proceed along the Scharster Rijn to the bascule bridge $\frac{1}{2}$ mile S of Scharsterbrug. There are mooring stages on each side. It opens: Mon–Sat 9–12, 13–17, 18–20h; Sun, hols 9–12, 14–17, 18–20h. At Scharsterbrug village there is an *ophaalbrug* which opens during the same times as the bridge just passed; there are mooring stages for a shopping stop on both sides of it.

Two miles N, Jachthaven de Woudfennen has box moorings, showers and a fuelling stage; and leads into a lake called Langweerder Wielen.

Langweerder Wielen

If your mast clearance is less than 12 m you can take a short-cut to the Sneekermeer by following the buoys NE for a mile to the 12 m fixed bridge over the Oudeweg. There is an opening bridge just beyond the fixed one, which has the same opening hours as at Scharsterbrug. Continue for 2 miles via the Noorder Oudeweg into the S end of the Sneekermeer, called the Goingarijpster Poelen.

If your mast is too high for that way, leave the lake via the Langweerder Vaart at its NW end. There is a mooring place on the E side of the entrance to the Langweerder Vaart. Beware of a ferry at De Brekken. There are more mooring places beyond, N and S of the junction of the Slingerrak and Geeuw. Continue to the N end of the Langweerder Vaart where it joins the buoyed channel of the Prinses Margrietkanaal and proceed NE into that part of the canal called the Westerbrugsloot. This has a bascule bridge between kms 74 and 73 which opens: Mon–Fri 8–21h; Sat 8–20h; Sun, hols 9–12, 14–17, 18–20h. From the bridge continue for a mile into the Modderige Geeuw and thence into the Sneekermeer at the entrance to the Houkesloot. The latter waterway goes direct to the town of Sneek.

An alternative route out of the Langweerder Wielen is W via that part of the Johan Frisokanaal called the Janesloot. It leads through an *ophaalbrug* to the N end of the Koevordermeer and the Prinses Margrietkanaal. The bridge opens: Mon–Sat 9–12, 13–17, 18–20h; Sun, hols 9–12, 14–17, 18–20h. From the N end of the Koevordermeer there is a choice of continuing W or N. The W route goes along the Johan Frisokanaal towards the Heegermeer and thence, as described before, back to Stavoren via the Fluessen; or via the Nauwe Wijmerts to Woudsend; or via the Wijde Wijmerts to IJlst and Sneek. The N route follows the Prinses Margrietkanaal to the Houkesloot and Sneekermeer as before. However it offers an interesting circular diversion into another pair of small lakes called the Witte and Zwarte Brekken, where there are plenty of mooring places in a very pleasant sailing area. On the Ooster Wijmerts, beware of a farm ferry by its junction with the Modderige Rijd.

Langweer

Before leaving the Langweerder Wielen there is a worthwhile diversion to the village of Langweer at the S end of the lake. It is a small place with a tiny harbour where you can moor to the quayside, and it makes a useful shopping stop as there are two supermarkets, butcher, baker, post office and vvv in the village. Toilets and showers are available at the camping site nearby. Just NW of the village, beyond the camping site, Jachthaven Leyenspolder has all facilities and a launderette.

Workum to the Lakes

Yachts with a draft of more than 2 m cannot use this route, but all the lakes and towns described in this chapter are accessible from Workum. (The entrance to Workum and opening times of its lock and three town bridges are covered in Chapter 10.) From the IJsselmeer proceed through the lock, then the Zuiderbrug, Bagijnebrug and Noorderbrug. A fee is payable in the lock for passage through the town, and again if you return the same way. The first lake is only 2 miles from Workum.

A small marina on the E side of the Noorderbrug on the S bank has showers and diesel. The next bridge, less than $\frac{1}{2}$ mile away, is a bascule bridge open: Mon–Sat 8–12, 13–17, 18–20h; Sun, hols 9–12, 14–17, 18–20h. There are mooring stages on each side. The last bridge before the lakes crosses the Klitrak about $\frac{1}{4}$ mile from the last one; it is a railway swing bridge which is manually operated and opens daily 6–20.45h. There is a marina on the W side of this bridge at the S bank, where it is possible to moor while waiting for the bridge; but there are no mooring places for boats waiting on the E side, and this can cause some difficulty if there is a strong following wind. Once through the railway bridge continue for a mile along the Lange Vliet to a tiny lake called Zandige Grons. From here there is a choice of turning N for the Vlakke Brekken, Oudegaaster Brekken and village of Oudega; or continuing E into the Zand Meer and Grote Gaastmeer. From the latter a channel leads into the Fluessen and Heeger Meer, wherefrom it is possible to return to Stavoren or proceed to Sneek and the Sneeker Meer; or return to Lemmer via Woudsend, the Sloter Meer and Sloten.

Oudega

At the end of the Lange Vliet turn N into the Grons and proceed for $\frac{1}{2}$ mile to the Vlakke Brekken lake. A pleasant diversion at its entrance offers a mile of eastbound sailing if the wind is favourable. There are some mooring places along the S bank at each end of the Ate Gracht. The Vlakke Brekken leads N for a mile into the Oudegaaster Brekken, which extends E for a mile to Oudega. The whole area provides good sailing and is less crowded than most other lakes.

The mooring stage at Oudega is on the S bank at the SE corner of the Oudegaaster Brekken, just E of the camping site. Showers (coin) are available at the camp site. The village has two small supermarkets, a vvv and post office, and a take-away snack bar. It is not possible to proceed beyond Oudega and continuation of your cruise necessitates returning to the Zandige Grons and then E into the Zand Meer and Grote Gaastmeer.

Grote Gaastmeer

From the Zandige Grons turn E into a lake which consists of two parts called the Zand Meer and Grote Gaastmeer. The island of Sont between the two has nice mooring places on all sides and an extensive grassy play area for children. There are many more pleasant bankside mooring spots all round the Zand Meer and W side of the Grote Gaastmeer. A channel from the E end of the latter leads to the village of Gaastmeer but it is difficult to find a vacant mooring place there. The SE end of the Grote Gaastmeer leads via the Inthiema Sloot into the Fluessen and thence to the rest of Friesland.

Makkum to the Lakes

Entry to Makkum from the IJsselmeer and passage through the town was described in Chapter 10. It is possible to go from Makkum via the Van Panhuyskanaal to the old city of Bolsward and then via the Bolswardervaart to IJlst and Sneek, a total distance of 12 miles. Alternatively, instead of turning N to Bolsward, turn S at Tjerkwerd to join the route from Workum to the lakes by the railway bridge over the Klitrak. A disadvantage of the routes from Makkum to Bolsward or Workum is their restricted Sunday bridge opening, which is confined to morning and evening. Furthermore, none of the routes from Makkum are open to yachts drawing more than 2 m.

Inland route from Germany to Belgium

For fixed-mast yachts, the inland route from Germany to Belgium passes through Friesland on its way to the IJsselmeer. The Dutch ends of this route are Delfzijl on the River Ems, which forms the German border, and Terneuzen on the Westerschelde.

From Delfzijl the Eemskanaal leads to Groningen, and thence via the Reitdiep into the Lauwersmeer *(fig. 38)*. This lake is also accessible from the Waddenzee through a lock at Lauwersoog. From the Lauwersmeer the Dokkumergrootdiep leads to Dokkum and thence via the Dokkumer Ee to Leeuwarden. Here the route continues via the Van Harinxmakanaal to Harlingen, or via Fonejacht and the Prinses Margrietkanaal to Lemmer. For yachts without a mast, a shorter route from Groningen to Lemmer is via the Van Starkenborghkanaal which joins the Prinses Margrietkanaal near Fonejacht.

From Harlingen or Lemmer the route crosses the IJsselmeer to Amsterdam, and continues to Terneuzen via the routes described in Chapters 3 to 9. At Terneuzen the canal to Ghent links the Dutch, Belgian and French canal systems, but masts must be lowered when Ghent is reached.

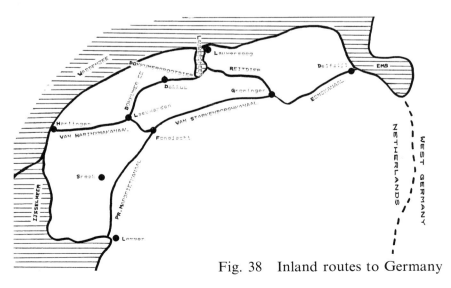

Fig. 38   Inland routes to Germany

Glossary

The following words are found in the Almanak and charts, and on signposts along the waterways; others may be helpful ashore. The letters IJ as in *vrij* are pronounced as in 'fry'.

DUTCH	ENGLISH
aanlegplaats	berth, mooring place
achter	aft
afgesloten	closed
afval	rubbish
alleen	only
anker	anchor
arts	doctor
bakboord	port side
basculebrug	bascule bridge
bediening	opening times
beneden	below
benzine (be.)	petrol
berm	obstruction
betonde	buoyed
betonning	buoyage
beweegbare brug	opening bridge
bezet	occupied, in use
bezoekers	visitors
binnen	inner
blauw	blue
boei	buoy
boot (boten)	boat(s)
bootmotorhersteller	marine engine repairer
boven	above
brug (bruggen)	bridge(s)
bruggeld	bridge dues
buiten	outer
diep	deep, or channel
diepte	depth
dieselolie (die)	diesel

doodtij	neap tide
doorvaarthoogte	vertical clearance
Douane	Customs
douche	shower
draaibrug	swing bridge
drinkwater	drinking water
duiker	diver
eiland	island
en	and
fiets(en)	bicycle(s)
gat	inlet, gut
geel	yellow
geen	no
geld	money
gesloten	closed
getijtafel	tide table
gevaar, gevaarlijk	danger, dangerous
goed	good
gracht	small canal
groen	green
groot	big
havengeld	harbour dues
havenkantoor	harbour office
havenmeester	harbourmaster
hefbrug	lifting bridge
hefkraan	crane
hier	here
hoogte	height
hoogwater	high water
ingang	entrance
jacht (en)	yacht(s)
jachtclub	yacht club
jachthaven	yacht harbour, marina
jachtwerf (*jachtwerven*)	boatyard(s)
kaart	chart
kabel	cable
kabel pont	cable ferry
kanaal	canal: VHF channel
kantoor	office
klein	small
korte	short
koud	cold
laagwater	low water
lang	long
langzaam	slow

lengte	length
ligplaats	overnight berth
geen –	no mooring
– prive	private berth
links	left
loods	pilot
marifoon	VHF radiotelephone
meer (meren)	lake(s)
meerboei	mooring buoy
meeren	moor
melden	report
motorbrandstof	fuel
naar	to
niet	not
nieuw(e)	new
noord(n.)	north
oever	bank
olie	oil
ondiep	shallow
oost(o.)	east
ophaalbrug	lifting bridge
oud(e)	old
overnachting	overnight
passanten	visitors
pontonbrug	opening pontoon bridge
prive	private
rechts	right
reddingsboie	lifebuoy
reddingsboot	lifeboat
reddingvest	life jacket
rood	red
schip (schepen)	ship(s)
schutsluis	tidal lock
slang(sl.)	hose
slecht	bad
sloot	drainage canal
sluis (sluizen)	lock(s)
sluisgeld	lock dues
snel	fast
snelheid	speed
spoorbrug	railway bridge
spoorweg	railway
springtij	spring tide
strijken	to lower
stuurboord	starboard
tandarts	dentist

te	at
te huur	for hire
toegang	admittance
ton	navigation buoy
tot	to
uit	out
uitgang	exit
vaargeul	fairway
vaartuig	vessel
vaarwater	navigable channel
vaste brug	fixed bridge
veer	ferry
verboden	forbidden
—*aan te leggen*	mooring prohibited
—*ankerplaats*	anchoring prohibited
verkeersbrug	road bridge
vlag	flag
vlot	raft
vlotbrug	opening pontoon bridge
vluchthaven	refuge harbour
voetganger	pedestrian
vrij	free, vacant
vuilnis	rubbish
warm	hot
wasgelegenheid	washing facilities
wassalon	launderette
weerberichten	weather forecast
werf (werven)	yard(s)
werk in uitvoering	works in progress
wit	white
zeilmaker	sailmaker
ziekenhuis	hospital
zuid(z.)	south
zwart	black
zwembad	swimming pool
zwemmen verboden	swimming forbidden
zwemvest	life jacket

General Index

Geographic Index

Main references are printed in bold type. The Dutch equivalent of y is IJ, and words beginning with IJ are accordingly placed in the index as if they began with y. VHF channels are given in brackets; and places with launderettes are indicated by (L).

172